DISCIPLESHIP 201

BY
GLENN SHAFFER

TWOWORDS
2300 SOUTHAVEN RD
CLAREMORE, OK
(918) 341-1765
TWOWORDS.TV
GLENNSHAFFER.TV

Table of Contents

Acknowledgements

A special note of appreciation is in order for those who have assisted me in many ways to finish these lessons. First of all, thanks to my wife for the evenings that I spent at the office to make deadlines and for her continual encouragement to write. I am deeply indebted to her keen ability to edit and time given to this project. I extend a big appreciation to our congregation for continuing to embrace a team ministry of pastors that has allowed me to commit to these long periods of writing and to our pastor/elders who carried extra loads. Thanks to our office staff, members, and a fellow pastor who has helped to proofread each page. Much work goes into producing even the simplest of writings, so I must share not only the work but also the credit.

Thanks to many church members who encouraged and field-tested these lessons through their feedback each week in the first classes.

May these lessons strengthen the body of Christ for years to come.

Welcome to Your New Walk

The Bible often speaks of our Christian life as a walk. That is because it is not stagnant but progressing. Your life in Christ is your new walk.

At this point, you should have completed *Christianity 101*. During those six weeks of lessons, you learned about your new life in Christ. Now you will advance in your Christian walk through *Discipleship 201*. Hopefully, you have recently attended a weekend spiritual retreat where you were taught of God's love, forgiveness, and His healing power in your life. Now it's time to walk out discipleship.

This book, *Discipleship 201*, is designed to help you take the next steps in your growth to spiritual maturity. It is intended for a classroom setting with daily devotions and homework. The purpose of the material is to build upon your foundation and bring you into an overcoming life in Christ. Each week that you attend this *Discipleship 201* class, you will cover the material you have studied that week. You will be asked to memorize two verses each week as well as study your daily devotional and class work. (See the appendix for your weekly memory verses.)

Your Christian walk will be affirmed and strengthened as you grow. Your maturity in Christ is important. That is why we want to do everything we can to see you become all that Christ has purposed for you.

These lessons are written so they build upon the previous lesson with the theme of an overcoming life. It is important that you follow through on each week's class and instruction. The discipline that you are developing now will be a key to your ongoing victories.

May God bless you as you grow in Christ.

Overcoming the World

Being a disciple involves being an overcomer. In this *Discipleship 201*, you will learn how to overcome in every area of your life. This week we learn about the world and how to live victoriously in this world rather than being entangled with it. Understanding this aspect is one of the first steps to being a disciple of Jesus Christ.

Becoming a Disciple

A disciple is a person who is fully committed as a follower of Christ. It means you are a true student of Christ's, allowing Him to work His will in your life. For you to be a disciple means that you will follow Jesus by growing in Him, understanding your gifts and ministry to serve others, and functioning in that capacity in a local gathering of believers, called the church. Being a disciple is a maturing process of a believer. It starts with believing in the Lord Jesus Christ, but it continues by following Christ's commands in every area of your life.

You are embarking on a new way of living. This is a walk of faith that will last the rest of your life. Your life is now hidden in Christ. As Paul wrote, "I have been crucified with Christ and I no longer live, but Christ lives in me. The life I live in the body, I live by faith in the Son of God, who loved me and gave himself for me" (Gal 2:20). The key words are, "the life I live in the body." Being a disciple is walking out the will of God in your body. What Christ has done for you legally in giving you right standing with Him, is now to be worked out experientially. That is why Paul writes, "put on the new self, created to be like God in true righteousness and holiness (Ephesians 4:24). Being a disciple is putting on the new self that never existed before. You are now a new creation made in His likeness and to walk that out in your daily life is to be a disciple. It requires your all.

Read the following passage very carefully. This is what Jesus said about being a disciple of His. He plainly states that unless you give up everything, you cannot be His disciple.

> *If anyone comes to me and does not hate his father and mother, his wife and children, his brothers and sisters—yes, even his own life—he cannot be my disciple. And anyone who does not carry his cross and follow me cannot be my disciple. Suppose one of you wants to build a tower. Will he not first sit down and estimate the cost to see if he has enough money to complete it? For if he lays the foundation and is not able to finish it, everyone who sees it will ridicule him, saying, "This fellow began to build and was not able to finish." Or suppose a king is about to go to war against another king. Will he not first sit down and consider whether he is able*

with ten thousand men to oppose the one coming against him with twenty thousand? If he is not able, he will send a delegation while the other is still a long way off and will ask for terms of peace. In the same way, any of you who does not give up everything he has cannot be my disciple. (Luke 14:26-33)

What Does It Take to Be a Disciple?

1. Jesus must be first in your life. Jesus knew that for the Jews to accept Him they would have to count the cost. It could even include being disinherited from their families. That is why He said that even family members could not come between you and your obedience to follow Christ. Jesus does not mean that we are to maliciously hate our family; He is simply calling us to make Him the number one priority to be a disciple. That goes for your own life as well. Your desires must be submitted to God.

2. You must take up your cross. To take up your cross is to deny yourself. It is an important aspect of being a disciple. One day, Jesus began to tell His disciples that He must go to Jerusalem and suffer many things and be killed and be raised from the dead on the third day. Peter did not like what he heard and took Jesus aside and rebuked Him and said that would never happen. Jesus turned to Peter and said, "Get behind me, Satan! You are a stumbling block to me; you do not have in mind the things of God, but the things of men" (Matthew 16:23).

The things of men come from the "world," which comes from Satan. Jesus spoke opposing and denouncing Peter's thoughts and words. Then Jesus said to His disciples, "If anyone would come after me, he must deny himself and take up his cross and follow me. For whoever wants to save his life will lose it, but whoever loses his life for me will find it" (Matthew 16:24-25).

To deny yourself does not mean to punish or inflict pain, but it means to submit your will and thoughts to God's way of thinking as if your-self life does not exist. Up to this point, you have learned to live your life for yourself.

Before going to the cross, Jesus was arrested. Peter, one of His disciples, was in the crowd at the time and a girl began to say that Peter was with Jesus. Peter responded that he did not know Jesus (Luke 22:57). Peter denied Jesus. To deny self is similar. You are saying, "I don't know that person." Denying yourself may involve denying things, but that is not what Jesus meant. Neither does it mean denying your self-worth or your emotional feelings.

In Greg Ogden's book, *Discipleship Essentials*, he states, "To deny yourself means to deny your self-lordship. It is saying—'I do not know "Lord Me"—I do not bow down to him or her anymore.'"[1] Where you have lived for yourself, now you are living for Christ. This is what Jesus meant when he said you must deny yourself. You have been crucified with Him, and you no longer live.

---

1 Greg Ogden, *Discipleship Essentials A Guide to Building Your Life in Christ* (Downers Grove, IL, InterVarsity Press, 1998), 28.

3. You must count the cost. Being a disciple is a serious and committed aspect of the life of a Christian. Many believers fail to move on to being a disciple because they are not willing to submit to the disciplines of following Christ. They enjoy the grace of Christ for redemption, but they are hesitant to get too serious. They may be afraid of becoming fanatical, but most often their resistance is due to strongholds from their past life where deep hurts and wounds have left them fearful of commitment. They want to hold onto the world rather than become a sold-out Christian.

Jesus said you must count the cost before you start the journey. That is why you have been asked to participate in a small group and be accountable with your life. Each person has a unique cost, but be assured; everyone has a cost. Have you counted your cost? You have accepted this discipleship course because you want to go all the way with God. Pause now and pray. Let God know that you are going to take the next steps. Ask Him for strength to take these steps.

4. You must give up everything. Did Jesus really say that? He not only said that, but he presents an interesting paradox. He said that if you try to save or keep your life, you will lose it; but if you lose your life for His sake, you will find it (Matthew 16:24-25).

When you give up everything, you are turning your life, thoughts, money, job, friends, relationships, talents, your body, your family, and your future over to God. Some people want to hold on to certain parts of their life. They are not willing to take the risk to see if Jesus is real in every area. Their reluctance keeps them from becoming disciples. They have not learned to trust God. They still want to be in charge of their own life. They have believed a lie that says if they trust God they will miss out on the best in life. Before long they have become snared with the cares of life. While they started out excited about Jesus, they soon became sidetracked. Being a disciple will teach you how to overcome three areas in your life, (1) the world, (2) the devil, and (3) sin. We will cover each of these areas over the next few lessons.

Application

1. In your own words describe what it means to be a disciple.

   you follow after Jesus
   you say to your self how can I
   serve others & Jesus is your 1st Love

2. What does it take to be a disciple?

   1) _Sell out to Jesus_
   2) _listen_
   3) _pray_
   4) _worship & praise_

3. Read Luke 14:26-33. Read it several times. What stands out to you the most about what Jesus said?

   verse 26

4. Check which of the following will be the hardest for you to turn over to Christ?
   • Your time
   • Your friends
   • Your relationships
   • Your money
   • Your family
   • Your thoughts
   • Your will
   • Your talents
   • Your entertainment
   • Your hobbies
   • Your body
   • Your mouth
   • Your future

Now pray over each area you checked. Ask the Holy Spirit to give you the desire and ability to trust Jesus completely. Remember what you seek to keep you will lose, but what you give up for Christ you will gain.

What is the World?

If you are a new Christian, you are probably excited about what has been happening in your life. No doubt, you may be somewhat amazed that many things that once had your attention, and were the center of your life, seem less important now. Even activities that are not considered wrong or sinful may have changed in your life because you are immersed in this new walk.

What will be an even bigger surprise for you is that some people who have been Christians for a long time may not share the height of your joy. At one time they were excited and on fire for God, but today their life may seem to be without the joy of the Lord. They have lost the excitement that you now possess. They may discourage you by their lack of zeal concerning what is going on in your life. These are Christians who have been overcome by the world.

Overcoming the world in your new Christian walk will be one of the most important aspects of your walk as a disciple. Even if you are entering this discipleship study as someone who has been a Christian for a long time, this subject is just as much for you.

When we speak of the world, we are talking about the philosophies, systems of operations, ideas, and ways of doing things that are outside of God's will. This includes people and activities that operate independently from the laws of God. In the Bible, there are several uses of the word *world*. It can mean the created order of things. However, it most often refers to the system and way of life that opposes God. The Bible says:

> *Do not love the world or anything in the world. If anyone loves the world, the love of the Father is not in him. For everything in the world—the cravings of sinful man, the lust of his eyes and the boasting of what he has and does—comes not from the Father but from the world.* (I John 2:15, 16)

Three aspects make up the world: (1) the things that attract the appetites of men (physical), (2) the things that appear attractive (mental), and (3) vain assurance in one's own ability (what others think about us).

Paul, an apostle, refers to the principles of this world as hollow and deceptive philosophies. He wrote to the church in Colossae warning them saying, "See to it that no one takes you captive through hollow and deceptive philosophy, which depends on human tradition and the basic principles of this world" (Colossians 2:8).

John, an apostle, wrote that those who oppose Christ are from the world and speak from the viewpoint of the world (1 John 4:5). So, we can say that the world has a viewpoint that opposes God. People in the world live with a worldview opposite of what a Christian has. That is where you have been and lived, before becoming a Christian. Paul explains that before becoming a Christian, we were following the ways of this world influenced by this present age. We lived in accordance with the prince of the power of the air, Satan, the spirit who is now at work in the disobedient or the unbelieving, who fight against the purposes of God (Ephesians 2:2).

Sin and the World

It should be pointed out that sin and the world are two different things. Both defile your life and are against God, but they do so in different aspects. The defilement of sin is personal and immoral. Even the sinner often knows he is doing wrong. Only the hardened sinner will support sin and say what he is doing is okay (Rom 1:28). The world is more subtle and refined and often appears beautiful and acceptable. Both the world and sin are unacceptable in the sight of God. It is just as crippling to be overcome by the world as to be contaminated by sin. It is possible for a believer to sin, yet not be caught up in the world. However, if one is overcome by the world, he is certainly entangled by sin and will find it impossible to live the life of a disciple. If one loves the world, he becomes an enemy of God (James 4:4). If Satan influences a believer to be a lover of the world, then he can have greater influence over that individual because that person's way of life, philosophies, and standards will oppose God. That person will be more concerned about their own pleasures, and what people think of them than what God thinks. A worldly man is without the fear of God. The worldly view of life is often justified and accepted in our culture and thus takes the place of God's perspective on life. Your worldview has significant implications on your life.

A person caught up in the world will allow it to erect strongholds in his or her mind, so his confidence will be in the world for provision, protection, and pleasure. Such a person may judge and charge God foolishly. God desires to be the one to satisfy you with pleasure, provision, and protection. The world usurps God's place and hinders you from honoring God. When a man thinks he determines his existence, fulfillment, and provision, he becomes driven by the world. That is why the scripture says, "If anyone loves the world, the love of the Father is not in him" (1 John 2:15).

If the love of the Father is not in him, that person will reject the things of God. If you seek your own pleasure apart from God, even good can become worldly. Remember, God, desires for you to have pleasure. It is not His plan to take that away from you, but He desires to be the source of that pleasure. Even in the Garden of Eden God created things that were pleasant to the eyes (Gen 2:9). It is not pleasure that God opposes, but rather mankind running after people, activities, and things that usurp God's place in one's life in to have pleasure.

Jesus experienced this temptation when the devil tempted Him in the wilderness by taking him to the top of the mountain and showing Him all the kingdoms of this world and their splendor. Satan said the kingdoms of the world were given unto him and he offered them to Jesus if He would bow down and worship him. Jesus came back with the word of God, "Away from me, Satan! For it is written: 'Worship the Lord your God, and serve him only'" (Matthew 4:10).

The devil's scheme was to get Jesus to pursue the splendor of the world and thus bring Jesus subject to himself. That is still a method of operation against you as a Christian. Jesus' response must be your response. You must be full of the Scripture to counter the temptations that the world sets before you. Later Jesus was given complete dominion over everything. He had to go the Father's way of the cross to receive the kingdoms of this world and not the shortcut offered by Satan. Being a disciple is going the way of the cross and not the way of the world. That takes trust in God. It takes a maturing Christian to identify the world and its bondage. Sin comes about when you give in to temptation birthed from your desires, but the world infiltrates through philosophies, concepts, and ideas that may appear to be acceptable and good but oppose the nature of God.

A person may even believe his way of thinking is only progressive, enlightened, and tolerant, when in fact he could be entertaining the world. That is not to say that Christians are to be closed-minded, judgmental, and non-accepting, but you must depend upon God's standards and not upon your way of thinking when being a disciple. Our way of thinking can often be entangled with the world and lead us astray.

That is where God's Word comes into the picture. A Christian's viewpoint must be reasoned from the Bible. The Word of God is alive and powerful and is able to judge the thoughts and attitudes of the heart (Hebrews 4:12). That is why you must guard your heart. The world entices the mind and heart. The more your heart is given to God, the less you will be attracted to the world. It is a journey of spiritual growth. Paul said it this way, "Do not conform to the pattern of this world but be transformed by the renewing of your mind. Then you will be able to test and approve what God's will is—his good, pleasing and perfect will" (Rom 12:2).

There is a pattern to the world. This pattern is the behavior, customs, and values of the world. Even a believer can conform to these worldly values without even being aware. That is why being a disciple must include the transformation of our thoughts and values. Without this transformation, it is possible for a Christian to live, think, and act as they did in their past life.

Application

1. When we speak of the "world," what are we talking about?

   how people live in the world

2. According to 1 John 2:15, 16, what are the three aspects of the world?

   lust

   flesh

   Pride

3. In what ways are sin and the world alike?

   The world says everything of
   to be your own you do what feels good

4. How are sin and the world different?

5. What did Jesus do when Satan tempted Him with the splendor of the world?

6. Ask the Holy Spirit to help you to see where the "world" has filtered into your way of thinking. This may not come quickly, but expect Him to begin to reveal these areas to you.

Satan and The World

Sin, Satan, and the world are closely connected. In today's lesson, we will address the part that Satan has as the prince of this world. It is important to understand that Satan does have a place of dominion, but it is limited and operates in sin and darkness. It is called the kingdom of darkness (Colossians 1:13).

The Bible calls Satan the prince of this world and the ruler of darkness (Ephesians 2:2; John 12:31). Paul wrote to the Corinthians saying, "The god of this age has blinded the minds of unbelievers so that they cannot see the light of the gospel of the glory of Christ, who is the image of God" (2 Corinthians 4:4).

The word "age" is sometimes translated as the world. The world is the total collection of all people, activities, and things that oppose God, but the age is just the present portion that we contact. Paul referred to his generation as "the present evil age" (Galatians 1:4). In Ephesians he tells the Christians that they once followed the "course," or ways of this world and of the ruler of the kingdom of the air, the spirit who is now at work in those who are disobedient (Ephesians 2:2).

Though Satan is the ruler of the "world," that must be understood as the system of life that opposes God and not the world of creation. He is not in charge of anything but darkness. Since he is the prince of darkness that is his place of dominion. The Bible tells us that we have been delivered from the kingdom of darkness and translated, or removed to, the kingdom of the Son (Colossians 1:13). Satan's portion is the world in all of its activities of sin and darkness.

With that in mind, we must remember what the Bible says. As King David wrote, "The earth is the LORD's, and everything in it, the world, and all who live in it" (Psalm 24:1). Satan is not in charge of the earth; God is. For Satan to have authority, he must influence those on the earth who live in darkness. That is why the scripture says that those in the world cannot understand the things of God. Their minds have been blinded. The Bible calls it the spirit of the world. As Christians, we have not been given the spirit of the world. Paul wrote, "We have not received the spirit of the world but the Spirit who is from God, that we may understand what God has freely given us" (1 Corinthians 2:12).

That is why you must ask God to show you where the world influences you. Where the world's influence is in your life, you will be more subject to temptations of the world and be led astray. Everyone who comes to Christ still has a non-Christian worldview. That is why our minds must be renewed. This is true for every single person who becomes a disciple. Being a disciple is growing in your understanding of God's perspective on life itself.

Entangled with the World

Paul had a team of workers that traveled with him and did the work of the ministry. Demas, one of his team members, became snared by the world and left Paul's ministry team. Paul explained, "For Demas, because he loved this world, has deserted me and has gone to Thessalonica" (2 Timothy 4:10).

The lure of the world must have been powerful to have that kind of effect on Demas. Demas became sidetracked from the ministry and purpose of God for his life. If that is true for this man in the Bible, just think how important it is for you to overcome the world. We are not told what happened to Demas. When Demas left Paul and went to Thessalonica, did he join up with the church there or did he just hide out in that worldly city? We don't know for sure, but if experience tells us anything, he probably stayed away from the Christians. What we do know about Demas is that he left his place in a very powerful ministry team, and walked away from the purpose of God for his life.

Have you ever seen individuals who claim to be Christians, and at one time they seemed very committed to God, yet today there is little difference in their lifestyle and those who are not followers of Christ? The problem is that they have been entangled with the world. We cannot question their salvation because eternal judgments belong to the Lord. We must give room for God's grace to sustain them, but it is difficult for those people to be free once they are overcome by the world. Peter writes about the problem of being overcome by the world: "If they have escaped the corruption of the world by knowing our Lord and Savior Jesus Christ and are again entangled in it and overcome, they are worse off at the end than they were at the beginning" (2 Peter 2:20). There is no one who is more miserable than a Christian who is overcome by the world. Their heart becomes hardened. They refuse to listen because they think they already know better. They live with shame. They may even find themselves opposing other Christians.

We are forgiven of our sins, but we must walk away from the world. We must guard our hearts against the philosophies, concepts, and ideas that oppose the very will of God. To walk away from the world is a figure of speech. You need not leave your job, family, or place where you live, but your thoughts, heart, and desires must be centered on God. What once held you dearly must now be subjected to Christ.

Jesus died for your sin, but He overcame the world. You have accepted Jesus' sacrifice for your sin, but you must walk out the victory over the world in everyday life. Though it is by the power of the Spirit that we overcome the world, it still requires hard choices and denying what we want and accepting God's will. That is part of being a disciple and following Jesus. Since Satan is the ruler of the world, it becomes extremely important that we determine to not come under his influence by being entangled with the world.

You can be born again, know some scriptures, and still become enticed with the world. If this takes place, you will find your heart being less tender towards the Holy Spirit, and you will find it easier to justify sin. If you become snared by the world, it is possible to even question the validity and relevance of God's word for your life today.

Some Christians have taken the wrong approach to this dilemma. They have taken the simplistic approach of withdrawing and becoming irrelevant to their world. They see themselves in constant conflict with people in the world. They speak of "us" and "them," thus separating themselves into a hostile mindset. They have forgotten that we do not wrestle with people but with spiritual forces. Paul said that we should not remove ourselves from people who are in the world (1 Corinthians 5:9, 10). Jesus told us to become a light to the world. Before going to the cross, Jesus prayed that we would not be taken out of the world but protected from the evil one while in the world (John 17:15). That is why it is so important to overcome the world even as Jesus did. John tells us, "The world and its desires pass away, but whoever does the will of God lives forever" (1 John 2:17). As you submit to Christ and the Word of God you will find the desires of the world passing away and the will of God living through you.

In the next lesson, we will address the proper means of overcoming the world and how Christ has made this provision available to you.

Application

1. What Scripture tells us that Satan is the god of this world?

   eph 2:2

   John 12:31

2. If the world is the total comprehension of people, activities, and things that oppose God, what do we mean by the "age?"

3. What does Satan's dominion include?

   anything that doesn't bring Jesus
   victory

4. Who was Paul's team member who deserted Paul for the love of the world?

   Demas

5. We are forgiven of our sin, but we must __turn__ away from the world.

6. Jesus died for your sin, but He __Overcame__ the world.

7. Tell God just how much you want to be free from the entanglements of the world. Look back at your lesson application from yesterday and see what you have written down concerning the areas in which you want to be free from the world. If God shows you more, then write those down as well.

8. Don't forget to be working on this week's memory verses located in the appendix at the back of this book.

Week One – Day Four

Victory Over the World

By now you should have a good idea of what the world is and how important it is for you to overcome. It is an essential aspect of being a disciple. Many Christians have become deceived because they did not learn this valuable truth.

These daily lessons are creating a regular devotional time in your life. It is essential to your spiritual growth. At this time in your Christian walk, you should have developed a regular time of prayer, Scripture memorization, and Bible reading. As time passes, you will realize just how much God's Word is getting into you. As you read, meditate, and memorize the scriptures, God's Word is changing your thoughts, ideas, and the way you look at life.

In today's lesson, you will learn that you were born for victory. God has provided the full means for you to walk in freedom and overcome the world. It is not something that you do on your own. Your victory is not through will-power.

When people speak of the world, they often end up talking about sin. Though sin and the world are two different things, they go together. Not only is Satan the god of this "world," those who practice sin are also of the devil, for the devil has sinned from the beginning (1 John 3:8). You may recall the scripture in 1 John 2:16, that identified the three aspects of the world: the lust of the flesh, the lust of the eyes, and the boastful pride of life. Though these things are in the world, notice how they appeal directly to the flesh.

Jesus Overcame the World

Before Christ came, even those who walked after God's laws were considered to be under the principles of the world (Galatians 4:3). The rest of the nations or people—often called Gentiles—were separated from God and excluded from the covenants of promise without hope and God in the world (Ephesians 2:12). Then Jesus came and revealed God to mankind. He walked on this earth as God in the flesh, fully man, yet fully God. As a man, He experienced temptations from the devil, enticements of the world, and the suffering of obedience. Jesus had to walk on this earth as a human, so that He could represent us before the Father. Jesus lived under the law of God and never broke the law not even once. He never sinned and never gave in to the temptations of the world. Before Jesus went to the cross, He declared to His disciples that He had overcome the world. Jesus said, "I have told you these things so that in me you may have peace. In this world you will have trouble. But take heart! I have overcome the world" (John 16:33).

This was good news for Jesus' disciples and you. The reason Jesus overcame the world was that there was no way for Satan to get an inroad into His life. Jesus resisted the lust of the flesh, the lust of the eyes, and the pride of life; therefore, Satan had no way of touching Him. Now we live our life in Christ to have the same victories.

When speaking of Jesus' fast-approaching death on the cross, He told His disciples that the "prince of this world is coming." He meant that Satan would be working through people like Judas, one of Jesus' disciples who betrayed Him. He knew the hour was coming when He would be crucified before the whole world and the prince of darkness would think that he had won a victory over Jesus. The truth of the matter was declared, however, when Jesus said, "I will not speak with you much longer, for the prince of this world is coming. He has no hold on me" (John 14:30).

The fact that the prince of this world had no hold on Jesus meant that Satan had no way of entangling Him. Jesus was saying that Satan had no power over Him and had no legal reason to get a hold of Him. This is significant for you because you are "in Christ," the devil or the world has no legal right to you.

You Were Born to Overcome

John asked the question, "Who is it that overcomes the world?" Then he answers it with, "Only he who believes that Jesus is the Son of God" (1 John 5:5). A few verses earlier, in 1 John 5:1, he established the truth that everyone who believes that Jesus is the Christ (the anointed one from God), is born of God. Then he says, "Everyone born of God overcomes the world. This is the victory that has overcome the world, even our faith" (1 John 5:4).

You were born for victory. Your victory is both present and future. It is a fact, and it is the truth. Those who are born of God overcome the world. This is part of your birthright. It is both a present truth and a promise. Faith speaks as if it is accomplished. It is the rest of the verse, "This is the victory that has overcome the world, even our faith." This victory "has" overcome the world. That is true because of what Jesus did. Now it is true for you because you believe in the Lord Jesus Christ. Your faith must now be in His completed work. Christ won the victory over the world, so have we. His life, death, and resurrection give us victory not only over sin but the world as well. Paul wrote, "Since you have died with Christ to the basic principles of this world, why, as though you still belonged to it, do you submit to its rules?" (Colossians 2:20).

All that oppose Christ are identified with the world. That is why John warned the Christians about those who do not accept Jesus Christ as God, who has come in the flesh or human form. He said they were from the world and speak from the viewpoint of the world (1 John 4:5). He said that every spirit that does not acknowledge Jesus is not from God and is of the spirit of the antichrist (1John 4:2-3). However, John does not stop there. He boldly proclaims, "You, dear children, are from God and have overcome them because the one who is in you is greater than the one who is in the world" (I John 4:4).

Stop and think about what John has written. The Holy Spirit in you is greater than the spirit that is in the world. With all the enticement and sway of the world, the Holy Spirit's influence over you is superior to the sway of the world.

You are not only born for victory, but you have the abiding presence of the Spirit of God guiding your thoughts, ideas, and philosophies. That is why you can declare that you have the victory over the world.

Application

1. Jesus came to reveal the Father. He was fully God and fully man. As man He experienced _temptations_ from the devil, _enticements_ of the world, and the _____ _suffering_ of obedience.

2. Why is it good news for you that Jesus overcame the world?

   that when we pass from this world we will go to heaven if we ask Jesus in our hearts

3. What did Jesus mean when He said, "The prince of this world is coming, but he has no hold on me?"

   because Jesus had never sinned so the devil had no hold on him

4. According to 1 John 5:1, who is born of God?

   everyone that believes he is the "son" of God

5. According to 1 John 5:4 who overcomes the world?

   we do through our victory & faith

6. There is a spirit in the world that opposes Christ. What is that spirit called in 1 John 4:2, 3?

   Antichrist

7. How can you know that God's Spirit has greater influence over your life? What verse tells you that truth? Write it out in your own words.

   1 John 4:4
   _3_

8. Meditate upon the power and influence of the Holy Spirit in your life. Where do you need His influence the most against the spirit of the world?

Your Cooperation, His Victory

Around 3000 years ago, David served as king of Israel. He had some very powerful men who fought for him in battle. Three of these men were known as David's mighty men. They did great exploits while fighting the enemies of God's people. One of these men was named Eleazar. One day these mighty men were with David, and they gathered in a battle against the Philistines. All the army of Israel withdrew and left David and these three fighters to defend Israel. Speaking of Eleazar, the scriptures say,

> *He stood his ground and struck down the Philistines till his hand grew tired and froze to the sword. The LORD brought about a great victory that day. The troops returned to Eleazar, but only to strip the dead.* (2 Samuel 23:10)

Can you imagine the effort that Eleazar put into the battle that day? He swung his sword so hard and so long that his hand stuck to the sword. He fought with all his might and struck down the enemy. The scripture declares, "The Lord brought about a great victory that day." Who won the victory? Did Eleazar and David's mighty men win? Or did the Lord bring about the victory?

This scenario is repeated throughout the Bible. Men gave great effort, but God is revealed as the one who brings the victory. It is God's way of showing His power through His creation. There can be no victory without the Lord, but God has chosen for you to put the sword in your hand and fight the battle.

These Old Testament stories of battles and victories are given to us to show how God fights our spiritual battles today. Just as Eleazar fought with all his effort, it was God who made him victorious; and that is true for you and your victory. Though Jesus has overcome the world, you are required to apply your faith to His completed work.

Your Sword of Victory

The Bible tells us that the Word of God is our sword of the Spirit (Ephesians 6:17). Since the spirit that is in the world is of the devil, you can use the same sword of the Spirit in resisting the world as you do against Satan. That is what Jesus did when He quoted the Word of God against the temptations of the devil and the splendor of the world. Jesus said, "It is written," and then He quoted the scripture.

Your Sword and Your Mind

Since the world is made up of thoughts, ideas, and philosophies that oppose God through people, activities, and things, then you must apply the sword to your thoughts. Paul knew how these patterns could influence us. That is why he wrote, "Do not conform any longer to the pattern of this world, but be transformed by the renewing of your mind. Then you will be able to test and approve what God's will is—his good, pleasing and perfect will" (Romans 12:2).

These philosophies and thoughts from the world attempt to bring you into the pattern of this world. Nothing will prevent that from happening except the renewing of your mind with the Word of God. To renew your mind means to renovate or to rebuild. For years you have thought, talked, and believed like the world. Now you are a new creation, but you still have thoughts that follow the pattern of the world. Even Christians who have served the Lord for a long time can fall back into this pattern.

Your daily devotions and meditations on God's Word are the key to victory. Without renewing of the mind, it is impossible for you to believe that God knows best for you. Without God's Word, you will not only find it hard to know God's will, but you will oppose it because of the worldly thoughts that are still resident in your mind. Without this renewal, you will not be able to trust God for your life. That is why you must rebuild your thought life. Old fantasies, mental pictures, and ways of dealing with issues in life will constantly resurface.

How you treat your family and friends is based on a mental picture you have of how things were for you. You will even find yourself making decisions and taking actions in keeping with what you saw in others whom you admired before becoming a Christian.

Immoral decisions that God opposes might be in your life until you realize what God's Word says about those situations. You must trust the Holy Spirit. He will reveal to you these truths, but it requires the written Word to be your standard. Without the Word of God as our final standard, we all can be misled through deception.

You Have Everything You Need

Since you were born to overcome the world, God plans for you to walk in that victory. That is why He has provided everything that you need. Peter, an apostle, wrote:

> *His divine power has given us everything we need for life and godliness through our knowledge of Him who called us by His own glory and goodness. Through these He has given us His very great and precious promises so that through them you may participate in the divine nature and escape the corruption in the world caused by evil desires. (2 Peter 1:3, 4)*

It is not your ability or self-will but His divine power that is at work in you. It is the Word of God that is "His very great and precious promises." It is through these promises that we are given the opportunity to participate in the divine nature. When you came to Christ, you received this divine nature, but it requires the renewing of your mind to walk in or "participate in" this nature. By walking with God and growing in the knowledge of Him, you escape the corruption that is in the world. Your victory over the world will be in direct proportion to the time and effort that you put into rebuilding your thought life and worldly patterns that have been erected in your mind before coming to Christ.

If a Christian becomes careless and playful with sin and the world, he will awake one day to find corrupted patterns in his mind. Do you remember Demas? No doubt, this is how Demas forsook Paul and the ministry team. He is a biblical example of a Christian who allows worldly corruption in his mind. He soon loved the world more than he did the will of God.

You have a great, victorious life ahead of you. Christ has overcome the world and offered His victory to you through your new birth. You have the Word of God working in you even as you go through these daily lessons.

Read the following out loud:

- Christ overcame the world.

- I am born of God; therefore, I have overcome the world.

- I choose to renew my mind and not be conformed to this world.

- I have everything I need in God's Word to live out my victory over the world.

Application

1. Can you recall a recent victory where you put forth great effort, but you knew it was the Lord who gave you the victory? Write it out in general terms, particularly if it was of a private nature.

_____

_____

_____

2. Jesus resisted the devil's temptations by quoting the Word of God. Take some time and find the verses that apply to your temptations, and record them below. (You can ask for help from your mentor.)

Temptation   Scripture that applies

_____

_____

_____

_____

3. Identify patterns of this world that have already changed in your life because you have been renewing your mind. Name at least one of these.

_____

_____

_____

4. If the devil was able to snare you with the world, in what area would that be?

   • Lust of the flesh

   • Lust of the eyes

   • Pride of life

5. Do you know our two memory verses for this week? Practice saying them before you go to your class.

Overcoming Sin

The world, sin, and the devil are closely related and may seem like the same battle. However, we want you to see victory in your life over each area. Over the next few weeks, you will be challenged to build upon your present victories in Christ and allow the Holy Spirit to continue to bring you deeper into a separated life of holiness. I do not mean separated from people or life, but separated unto God for His pleasure. Being set apart for His service is sometimes called holiness, and other times it is referred to as sanctification, but for right now we will call it "overcoming the world, sin, and the devil."

What is Sin?

Sin is the violation of the law of God. John wrote, "Everyone who sins breaks the law; in fact, sin is lawlessness" (I John 3:4). One theologian describes sin by saying, "Sin is any failure to conform to the moral law of God in act, attitude, or nature. Sin includes not only individual acts such as stealing or lying or committing murder, but also attitudes that are contrary to the attitudes God requires of us."[2]

Sin is lawlessness or rejecting God's will. A person sins by doing what the law prohibits, or by disobeying God by omitting what He requires. In short, sin is disobedience. The literal translation is "missing the mark," or falling away from the standard. God's law is the mark, and when we transgress against his standard, we have sinned.

Sin is disobedience. It has been said that the center of all sin is selfishness. When a person puts his will higher than God's, it becomes hostile to God. The evil of sin lies in the fact that it is against God, even when the acts, thoughts, or words are against another person. When King David repented for his sin of adultery, murder, and lying, he understood this and prayed to God saying, "Against you, you only, have I sinned and done this evil in your sight" (Ps 51:4). Though it was clear that he had sinned against Bathsheba, her husband Uriah, and all of Israel, it was first and foremost against God.

In defining sin, *Nelson's Bible Dictionary* says, "Sin is not represented in the Bible as the absence of good or as an illusion that stems from our human limitations. Sin is portrayed as a real and positive evil. Sin is more than unwise, inexpedient, calamitous behavior that produces sorrow and distress. It is rebellion against God's law—the standard of righteousness."[3]

---

2 Wayne Grudem, *Systematic Theology An Introduction to Biblical Doctrine* (Grand Rapids, MI: Zondervan Publishing House, 1994), 490.
3 Nelson's Illustrated Bible Dictionary, (Thomas Nelson Publishers, 1986)

Adam, Sin, And You

How did sin enter the human race? Sin began for humanity in the Garden of Eden when Satan brought temptation to Adam and Eve, and they succumbed to his deceptions (Genesis 3:1-19). Satan came to Adam and Eve in the form of a serpent. Tempting Eve to question God, the serpent said, "Did God really say, 'You must not eat from any tree in the garden'?" Next, the serpent refuted God outright and said, "You will not surely die!" Eve listened and ate of the fruit and gave to her husband, and he too ate of the forbidden. In the day that Adam ate of the forbidden fruit, he died; he died spiritually as a result of disobedience. He died not for the maliciousness of an act, but an act of disobedience. At that time sin entered the human race. Paul explains, "Therefore, just as sin entered the world through one man, and death through sin, and in this way death came to all men, because all sinned" (Romans 5:12). As a result of Adam's sin, now all of mankind has sinned and received the sentence of death. A person is not a sinner because he sins, he is a sinner because he was born into Adam through the human race. Paul explains further:

> *Consequently, just as the result of one trespass was condemnation for all men, so also the result of one act of righteousness was justification that brings life for all men. For just as through the disobedience of the one man the many were made sinners, so also through the obedience of the one man the many will be made righteous.* (Romans 5:18, 19)

Jesus became the last Adam. In the same way that sin came to all men, righteousness now flows to those who are Christ's. In Christ, we have righteousness reigning in our lives, even more so than death once reigned under the first Adam. Christ became the last Adam and gives life. Paul explained the result when he wrote, "The first man Adam became a living being; the last Adam, a life-giving spirit" (1 Corinthians 15:45). He also said, "So that, just as sin reigned in death, so also grace might reign through righteousness to bring eternal life through Jesus Christ our Lord" (Romans 5:21).

All men without Christ are dead spiritually, meaning, not alive to God. They are not dead in the sense of not being able to reject or rebel against God, for they certainly do that by nature. However, they live in spiritual death unable to come to God. That is why mankind is called "dead in sin." Before you came to Jesus you were alive unto the world, self, and sin, but dead to God and alienated from His life (Ephesians 4:18).

Your condition was far worse than you can imagine. Without Christ, you were without hope. The Bible tells us that man in this condition is incapable of understanding the things of God because he is without the Spirit of God. Paul wrote to the Corinthians,

> *The man without the Spirit does not accept the things that come from the Spirit of God, for they are foolishness to him, and he cannot understand them, because they are spiritually discerned.* (1 Corinthians 2:14)

Paul writes to the Ephesians and reminds them that they were dead in their transgressions and sins walking after the ways of the world and Satan. Then he declares the wonderful event that took place when God brought forth His life in those who believe.

> *But because of his great love for us, God, who is rich in mercy, made us alive with Christ even when we were dead in transgressions—it is by grace you have been saved. And God raised us up with Christ and seated us with him in the heavenly realms in Christ Jesus, in order that in the coming ages he might show the incomparable riches of his grace, expressed in his kindness to us in Christ Jesus. For it is by grace you have been saved, through faith—and this not from yourselves. It is the gift of God.* (Ephesians 2:4-8)

The entire human race identifies with two men. The first Adam and the last Adam. Those who are dead in their trespasses and sins are still in the first Adam. They live subject to sin and are in bondage to their sinful nature. The second group of people identifies with the last Adam, who is Christ Jesus. They have been raised from their spiritual death and are alive unto Christ. Those who are in Christ are free from the bondage of sin. Christians may sin, but they are not under the reign of sin. When a Christian sins, it is by choice; a sinner sins by nature. When you come to Christ, you are no longer under the power of sin. Where sin once reigned in their bodies by the authority of the first Adam, that power has been destroyed through the sacrifice and death of Christ (Romans 5:17).

Give God thanks for delivering you from the power of sin.

Application

1. According to 1 John 3:4, what is sin?

   Conform to the moral law of God
   act attitude or nature

2. We may define sin as follows:

   going agaist God's law

3. Explain how sin came into the human race.

   in the garden w/ adam & Eve.
   disobedience

4. Give one scripture that tells us that by Adam's sin all have sinned.

   for all have sinned & come short of the
   glory of God

5. If death came by the first Adam, what was the result of the last Adam?

6. Ask the Holy Spirit to show you the seriousness of sin. Take time express your appreciation to Christ for your redemption from sin.

7. Go to the appendix at the back of the book and begin to memorize the first of the two memory verses for this week.

Identifying Sin

Today's lesson is designed to help you recognize sin and see how sin occurs. To walk in the victory that has already been provided for you in Christ, it is important for you to recognize sinful patterns that have developed or remain in your life since becoming a Christian.

God told Cain, the first murderer in the Bible, that sin was waiting at the door to attack him, but he must master it (Genesis 4:7). That is true for you as a disciple following Jesus. Even though sin no longer has any power over you and you are a new creation in Christ, there is nothing good in your flesh. Paul explains it by saying the sin principle is in him (Romans 7:17, 18). He says, I can decide to do what is right and cannot perform it. It shows us how dependent we are on the Holy Spirit. As long as we live in this fallen world, we will experience the weakness of our flesh and sin will always be close by. However, that does not mean that sin has power or reign over us now. It does not. That is our victory.

There are three ways in which a person can sin: thought, word, and action. Let's take a look at each one.

1) Thoughts of the heart—Religious leaders during Jesus' day believed they could be considered free from sin if they did not perform the actual act of sin. Jesus came along and told them that sin starts in the heart and thoughts of man. They became proud of their own righteousness, yet Jesus confronted them with their sin. This was not a new concept, however, because even the Ten Commandments forbade one to covet their neighbor's house, wife, servant, ox, donkey, or anything that belongs to the neighbor (Ex 20:17). Coveting comes from the heart. Jesus was reminding them that when a person thinks evil and holds it in his heart, it becomes sin. That is why He told them,

> *What comes out of a man is what makes him unclean. For from within, out of men's hearts, come evil thoughts, sexual immorality, theft, murder, adultery, greed, malice, deceit, lewdness, envy, slander, arrogance, and folly. All these evils come from inside and make a man unclean.* (Mark 7:20-23)

You cannot prevent thoughts from coming into your mind, but a Christian must not allow himself to dwell on sinful thoughts. Entertaining unholy thoughts long enough to stir your desires opens the door for that yearning to be realized in your heart. James says, when desire has been fulfilled, it brings forth sin (James 1:15).

Jesus explained how we could sin in our mind or heart concerning sexual lust and hate.

You have heard that it was said, "Do not commit adultery." But I tell you that anyone who looks at a woman lustfully has already committed adultery with her in his heart. (Matthew 5:27, 28)

Anyone who hates his brother is a murderer, and you know that no murderer has eternal life in him. (I John 3:15)

Sins of omission are considered sins of the heart. It is an act of disobedience. Anyone who knows the good he ought to do and does not do it, to him it is sin (James 4:17). Sins of rebellion, disobedience, bitterness, and unforgiveness obviously begin in the heart. Other sins may seem obvious, but some of these sins of the heart are difficult to recognize because of events or situations we find ourselves in life make it easy to justify.

2) **Words**—The Jewish leaders often tried to trap Jesus with His words. They were unable to do so because Jesus only spoke what He heard from the Father. Sinning with your mouth can happen with much subtlety. Before you know it, you have said something that you regret and may have been very damaging to someone's feelings or reputation.

The biblical admonition to guard against sinning with our tongue is enormous. Jesus begins by telling the Jewish leaders of His day,

But I tell you that men will have to give account on the day of judgment for every careless word they have spoken. For by your words you will be acquitted, and by your words you will be condemned. (Matthew 12:36-37)

Peter said,

For, "Whoever would love life and see good days must keep his tongue from evil and his lips from deceitful speech..." (1 Peter 3:10)

Paul wrote,

Do not let any unwholesome talk come out of your mouths, but only what is helpful for building others up according to their needs, that it may benefit those who listen. (Ephesians 4:29)

Nor should there be obscenity, foolish talk or coarse joking, which are out of place, but rather thanksgiving. (Ephesians 5:4)

But now you must rid yourselves of all such things as these: anger, rage, malice, slander, and filthy language from your lips. (Colossians 3:8)

James, the brother of our Lord, wrote that if a person were never at fault in what he said, that person would be a mature individual (James 3:2).

How do you sin with your mouth? From the Scriptures we see that sinning with our mouth occurs through cursing others, gossip, slander, lying, complaining, grumbling, flattery, obscenity, foolish talking, coarse joking, or using harsh words (James 3:9; 1 Corinthians 10:10). Paul gave the best instruction when he said, "Let your conversation be always full of grace and seasoned with salt" (Colossians 4:6).

3) **Actions**—Though you can sin in your heart without an "act" of sin, some sins do come to action. Sinning with your mouth is considered an action as well. When acts of sin occur, they often involve others. For example, if you lust in your heart, you have sinned against God; but if the act is carried out, then your transgression has broadened. Sometimes one act of sin can be against several people. This is true in the case of adultery. Not only is it a sin against the one with whom you are involved, but it is also a sin against the spouse. Sexual sins with an unmarried person can also be a transgression against their parents (Exodus 22:16, 17).

Though all sin has great consequences, sinning with our actions has the greatest impact on others. All sin is against God and can be considered equal in transgression against God's holiness, but some sins carry greater consequences. Obviously, sins in the heart can be confessed to God alone, but acts against others require confessing and asking for forgiveness from others.

Paul tells us there is one sin that is not like other sins. He writes, "Flee sexual immorality. All other sins a person commits are outside the body, but whoever sins sexually, sins against their own body (1 Corinthians 6:18).

In summary, sins can be identified as coming from thoughts of the heart, our mouth in what we say, and our actions toward God, ourselves, and others.

Application

1. What are the three ways in which a person can sin?

   thoughts of the heart

   words

   action

2. Jesus explained that what defiles a man is what comes out of him. According to Mark 7:20-23, what sins come out of a person's heart?

3. Explain a sin of omission.

4. According to Peter, "Whoever would love life and see good days must..."

5. Identify ten ways that you can sin with your mouth.

   filthy words

   talk about some one

6. When you sin with your actions, it often involves _____.

7. Ask the Holy Spirit to show you your heart. Ask Him to remind you to place a guard over your mouth. Tell God that you want your life to be free from patterns of sin.

Consequences of Sin

Sometimes Christians think they can ignore sin and it will produce little or no injury. Some may justify their sin as not being great or serious. Others who hear of God's wonderful message of grace and mercy may have a misunderstanding of His longsuffering and think that sin has little consequence. For whatever reason, a person may ignore his sin. This lesson is to reveal the consequences of sin and challenge you to address it through His grace and not become overwhelmed by it.

Your Position Vs. Your Progress

It is important that you not confuse your position with God with your spiritual progress. At times you may see that you are making real spiritual advancement, and then a few days later you wonder what has happened to you. This happens to all Christians. As you mature, you will recognize that your digressions will be shorter and with less depth of deviation. This is a process of your development and spiritual growth. You are moving towards spiritual maturity and Christ-likeness. If you remain spiritually healthy, you will continue this process all through your life. The real problem comes when Christians go long periods of time without a clear testimony of spiritual growth and change. When that occurs, it is evidence that they have not learned to overcome sin.

Your position or legal standing with God is in Christ. Therefore, when you sin as a Christian, your position does not change, and God does not stop loving you. God is displeased with sin, but God's displeasure is not a sign of a lack of His love for you but quite the opposite. That is why the writer of Hebrews tells us that God disciplines His children when they refuse to resist sin (Hebrews 12:1-11). He corrects us because He loves us. We are His children. God chastens you, but He does not kick you out of His family. Your legal standing with God is through the grace of Christ Jesus and not on your merit. It is a free gift (Ephesians 2:8-9). Your legal position is that you are the righteousness of God. However, John tells us that as Christians, if we claim that we have no sin, we deceive ourselves, and the truth is not in us (1 John 1:8). That is why you can know that your position is not based on your ability to live sinless, but in your adoption into the family of God. Jesus paid the price for all your sins past, present, and future. On the other hand, your progress is related to overcoming sinful patterns in your life. God's forgiveness and mercy do not mean that sin can be ignored in your life. If you allow known sin to remain in your life, it will adversely affect your progress and sensitivity to God.

Sinful Patterns and Your Progress

Occasionally a Christian may sin through speaking a wrong or acting sinfully. They quickly become sorrowful, ask forgiveness to all who were affected, and little damage will occur. Though all sin is serious, if that sin is not a pattern in the life of that Christian then progress is not hindered. When we speak of sinful patterns, we are not talking about occasional overt sin. We are referring to the works of the flesh that have become strongholds in our life. It keeps you from progressing in God. These patterns form character flaws and hindrances to your progress.

Sin Divides Your Loyalties

When you hold on to sin in your heart, then you have made something greater than God. The Bible tells us that when we do this, it hinders our prayers (Psalm 66:18; 1 Peter 3:7). It divides our loyalties. It becomes idolatry. It brings a war against your soul. That's right, sin wars against your soul. If you regard sin in your life, it is the same as welcoming the enemy of your soul. Peter wrote to the Christians and warned them of how important it was for them to abstain from sinful desires and its effect. He wrote, "Dear friends, I urge you, as aliens and strangers in the world, to abstain from sinful desires, which wage war against your soul" (1 Peter 2:11).

Three things happen in the life of a Christian whose loyalties are divided by holding onto sin. He becomes confused, unsettled, and dissatisfied. His relationship with God and others becomes difficult, scattered, and unsettled. His path becomes unclear. He has a sense of distance from God and often flounders for direction. That person often blames God, or others, for their condition. That person may even become restless and begin to look for the perfect job, spouse, church, or relationship. Since his loyalties are divided, all other relationships are affected. Conflicts arise with people around them and often with authorities. In reality, this person's conflict is not with man, but with God.

Sin Overshadows Your Freedom

There is a reproach to sin even if others do not know that you are involved in repeated sinful behavior (Proverbs 14:34; Psalm 39:8). You can lose your sense of freedom before God and become a slave to that sin. Paul warned us:

> *Don't you know that when you offer yourselves to someone to obey him as slaves, you are slaves to the one whom you obey—whether you are slaves to sin, which leads to death, or to obedience, which leads to righteousness?* (Romans 6:16)

Wayne Grudem explains the result of holding onto our sin and writes, "Our Christian life and fruitfulness in ministry are also damaged. Jesus warns us, 'As the branch cannot bear fruit by itself, unless it abides in the vine, neither can you, unless you abide in me' (John 15:4). When we stray from fellowship with Christ because of sin in our lives, we diminish the degree to which we are abiding in Christ."[4]

Sin Opens the Door to Darkness

Sin is of the devil and whoever does what is sinful is participating with the devil. It is not just your sin but also the whole world of darkness in which you are participating. For example, buying a pornographic magazine to satisfy your lust is more than your sin, it is also participating in that sphere of destruction. Using slander or gossip against someone is participating with the devil who is called the "slanderer." The Greek word for Satan is *diabolos*. It is translated two times as false accuser and one time as slanderer.

When we regard sin, we choose another authority over our lives. Satan only has authority over darkness, for he is called the ruler of darkness. To hold onto your sinful patterns is to participate with Satan and open the door in your life to darkness and deception.

Sin Can Affect Your Beliefs

When you hold onto your sin long enough, it can change your beliefs and move you from the principles of God's word (1 Timothy 4:1). This happens as a means of personal justification. You can end up accepting lies and think that God approves of your behavior. I have heard Christians say, "I know what God's word says, but I don't think God would want me to be unhappy." Their disobedience has become their deception. Since they insist upon their own will, their conscience does not bother them (1 Timothy 4:2). People will adjust their beliefs to accommodate their sin.

To overcome sin, you cannot ignore, justify, or tolerate it in your life. Knowing that we are no longer under the power or reign of sin should encourage us to walk in freedom from its bondage. That old way of life is not a part of our new nature in Christ. We know Christ has forgiven us and freed us from our sin, but we should never take it lightly. Knowing we are free in Christ should motivate us to walk in victory over it.

---

4 Wayne Grudem, *Systematic Theology An Introduction to Biblical Doctrine* (Grand Rapids, MI: Zondervan Publishing House, 1994), 505.

Application

1. In your own words, explain why it is important not to confuse your position with God with the progress you are making in spiritual growth.

   because it is not about you
   you are to bring glory to the father

2. Read Hebrews 12:1-11. Why does God discipline us?

   because he loves us

3. According to Hebrews 12, what happens with your position as a child of God when you have sinned? Are you kicked out of God's family?

   No you ask forgiveness & of course
   he forgives

4. Sin affects our spiritual progress. How does it divide your loyalties?

5. In your own words, explain why sin opens the door to darkness.

   because God is only light
   oppiste of light is dark it open
   you can't hear God if there is sin in your life
   all the time

6. Are there any sins that you have justified as being unimportant? If the Holy Spirit brought something to your remembrance during this lesson, stop and pray, submitting it to God. Tomorrow's lesson will help you to address it.

Addressing Sin

Years ago, there was popular hair cream that was sold in a tube. It was white like toothpaste and had similar color markings on the outside of the tube. On a few occasions, someone would accidentally grab the wrong tube and put hair cream on their toothbrush in the early morning light. It did not matter what they thought was on the inside; it was what came out when the tube was squeezed that mattered. So it is with your life. What is in your heart will come out when the pressures of life and temptation come against you. The key to victory over sin is understanding your righteous position in Christ and allowing the Holy Spirit to bear His fruit in you. The Holy Spirit brings forth the character of Christ. This comes about by being sensitive and obedient to the Holy Spirit.

Moses tells the children of Israel that if they will arm themselves and go to battle to drive out the enemy, they will receive their inheritance and their families will live in protection. Then he adds, "But if you fail to do this, you will be sinning against the LORD; and you may be sure that your sin will find you out (Numbers 32:23). Paul tells us these stories are written about Israel in the Old Testament for our example to keep us from setting our hearts on evil (1 Corinthians 10:6). Israel's natural enemies are an example of our spiritual enemies.

You can be a Christian while not living in your full inheritance. If you do not allow the Holy Spirit to you to maturity, you are living below what God has intended. Holding onto willful sin will catch up with you. Some people interpret the mercy and grace of God to mean that sin now does not matter today. It is true that Christ has dealt completely with our judgment and punishment for sin, but unaddressed sin has fruit and consequences in life.

Rest assured what is in your heart will eventually come out. You may have heard people excuse inappropriate words or actions by saying, "You just caught me on a bad day." Well, the truth is, those words or actions were already in their heart; it was circumstances or events that brought them out. It is what is in you that will come out. Sin will eventually adversely affect your life. What you allow to remain will eventually rise and defeat you (Galatians 6:7).

Confess and Repent of Sin

The first step is always to repent and confess your sins. This does not mean to get "saved" all over again. To repent is to change your mind. It is to do a one-eighty and head in the other direction. To confess means to say what God says about your sin. He wants you to say two things about your sin: the truth in full confession and the truth about His blood providing forgiveness of sin. Be honest and straightforward because He already knows your sin. The temptation is to make your sin seem less sinful or to punish yourself with words through self-deprecation or penance. Do neither. Simply tell God the wrong.

For example, "Father, I have hate in my heart for that person. I have carried it in my heart for these days. I have spoken against this individual. I know it is wrong, but I have ignored your Word to repent. I have been wrong. I receive your forgiveness. Oh God, thank You for the cleansing power of Your blood. You cleanse me from all unrighteousness."

Forgiveness and repentance are two different things. Forgiveness is immediate. It can be said that Jesus forgave us at the cross, but repentance must "work" in us. If the sin pattern is deep, repentance may take longer. Your way of thinking and responding may have become a pattern. Repentance can be compared to peeling an onion one layer at a time. Repentance comes in degrees. As you are more and more honest with yourself and God, He brings illumination to what needs to be corrected. Sin is ugly. That is why people deny their sin. They fear the pain of facing the truth more than the pain of their sin. Sometimes it takes being exposed for God to bring restoration; however, that happens only after a long period of God's dealings. Addressing sin is sometimes like finding the tip of an iceberg. It is not until repentance begins that you discover just how deep and powerful the stronghold is in your life. Once you see your sin as God sees it, it will work repentance, and repentance will bring victory.

Notice how the Corinthians learned the lesson of repentance. They became truly sorrowful for their sin. Godly sorrow brought them to a place where they wanted to be cleared of the matter. The Bible tells us Godly sorrow works repentance. They developed indignation or righteous anger for their sin. They were ready to see justice done. That is a good indication that repentance has come. Paul explained:

> Godly sorrow brings repentance that leads to salvation and leaves no regret, but worldly sorrow brings death. See what this godly sorrow has produced in you: what earnestness, what eagerness to clear yourselves, what indignation, what alarm, what longing, what concern, what readiness to see justice done. At every point, you have proved yourselves to be innocent in this matter. (2 Corinthians 7:10, 11)

"Worldly sorrow" brings death because it is a guilty conscience without genuine willingness to change. It is remorse for the hurt and discomfort that the sin caused for them and others. This type of sorrow does not see the sin as God sees it. A person with worldly sorrow may hate what he has done. He is sorry for lost goods, lost friends, and lost relatives. His guilt may be so strong that it becomes destructive, either by internal conflict or by an attempt to bring destruction to himself. That kind of sorrow only brings death.

You can tell if you have "worldly sorrow" or "godly sorrow" by determining if you are turning to God or away from God. Godly sorrow has the breach of God's law as its object where worldly sorrow has the sinner himself as the object. Godly sorrow brings hope. Worldly brings death. That is why a person with worldly sorrow will often attempt to blame others, deny the sin, or justify his action. His focus is to rid himself of guilt rather than turn from his sin to God. You cannot rid yourself of guilt, that is what the blood of Christ has done. His blood has freed us from a guilty conscience (Hebrews 10:22). If a Christian has a guilty conscience, they either have not understood the grace and forgiveness of God, or they are holding onto a hidden sin.

Renounce Sin

First, we receive forgiveness, but as we turn away from sin, we will want to renounce sin in our heart. That means we view sin as God does and we turn from it. Our heart must run away from sin (2 Timothy 2:22). This happens when we see how displeasing sin is to God. This is also part of the process of repentance.

Let repentance work in your heart so that you see the ugliness of that sin. Once you have confessed the sin and repentance is working in you, then renounce the sin and the desire for that sin.

For example, "Father, I thank You for Your forgiveness. I know You have removed my sins from me. I renounce the sin of _____ (place the sin in the blank). I choose to turn away from that transgression. I accept the help of the Holy Spirit to speak to me about this every time it comes up. Where I have chosen to sin now, I choose to be free from that sin."

When you confess acts of sin that involve others, then it requires the broader spectrum to be addressed. In other words, your confession must be as broad as your transgression. Some sins of action require restitution in addition to confessing of the sin. Not all sins are crimes, but all crimes are a sin. God made provision for certain crimes to have restitution. For example, if a person steals he must not only ask forgiveness from God and the person from whom he stole, but he must also make restitution to that individual (Exodus 22:1, 4). Making restitution can be a wonderful freeing activity in the life of a new believer.

Addressing sin requires all of these efforts when applicable.

1. Confess the sin.

2. Allow Godly sorrow to bring you to repentance.

3. Repent fully. When it is appropriate, one should seek forgiveness from others directly involved.

4. Make restitution when it is applicable.

Application

1. Explain in your own words what it means, according to this lesson, to confess you sins.

   To tell God your sin & tell him & repent

2. Forgiveness is immediate but _____ must "work" in us.

3. According to the lesson, explain "Godly sorrow."

   It brings repentence that will lead to Salvation

4. Explain "worldly sorrow."

   It will bring death, It is a guilt conscience decision un willing to change

5. Pray a prayer "renouncing" a particular sin with which you have struggled.

6. Name the four requirements to address sin.

   1) pride

   2) _____

   3) _____

   4) When applicable—_____

8. Work on the second memory verse for this week. Be prepared to recite both verses at your next class or meeting.

Overcoming Temptation

To be tempted means to experience a solicitation of evil or to be enticed to sin. The same word for temptation may also be translated "to try" or "to prove." God will never solicit us to evil or entice us to sin. There are times the scripture mentions that God tests or tries us (Exodus 16:4; 20:20; Deuteronomy 8:2). His testing is different than what comes from the flesh, the world, or the devil. The Bible tells us, "When tempted, no one should say, 'God is tempting me.' For God cannot be tempted by evil, nor does he tempt anyone" (James 1:13-15).

The temptation to sin comes from your flesh, the world, or Satan. However, all temptations begin with your desires. Even if Satan brings temptation, he must work with your desires. He cannot make you do something that you do not choose to do. Satan and his demons have been around for a long time. They know your weaknesses by watching you. Satan knows where you have fallen in times past. Once a weakness has been established, it becomes a stronghold in your life. The Book of James tells us how temptation works:

> *But each one is tempted when, by his own evil desire, he is dragged away and enticed. Then, after desire has conceived, it gives birth to sin; and sin, when it is full-grown, gives birth to death.* (James 1:14-15)

Temptation, in and of itself, is not an indication of evil in you. We know this is true because Jesus was tempted. He was tempted in every way just as we are; yet He never sinned (Hebrews 4:15). It is important that you remember this truth. Some people give in to temptation thinking they are spiritually weak because they are being tempted. They also give in too easily believing they will fail because of the past experience with temptation.

When temptation is strong you may think that you must give in; however, nothing is going to happen to you if you resist except victory. No matter how weak you think you are, you are not too weak to pass the test. God will not let that much temptation come to you. And, you are not the only one to have this same temptation. Paul explains this further:

> *No temptation has seized you except what is common to man. And God is faithful; he will not let you be tempted beyond what you can bear. But when you are tempted, he will also provide a way out so that you can stand up under it.* (1 Corinthians 10:13)

God will give you His ability to go through the temptation. Since Jesus suffered temptation, He is able to help you, knowing what you are going through (Hebrews 2:18).

Where Is the Influence?

When you are being tempted, take a moment and examine from which of the three areas your temptation is coming. Is it primarily your flesh, demonic, or the world?

The Flesh—If you have a pattern of sin you will have both the flesh and demonic influence in your life. Satan has influence through sin. If that is the case, it will be important for you to deal with both. Temptations gain more power the more you give into them. When you submit the members of your body to sin, it will eventually become your master (Romans 6:16).

Examine your environment. Are you seeing media, movies, or pictures that are influencing your flesh? Are you reading, talking, or thinking on subjects where you are vulnerable? Are your friends and relationships with others making your walk with God harder? Your environment, both mental and physical, has a lot to do with the temptations of the flesh. Your thought life is a key in this battle.

The World—Like temptations of the flesh, your struggle can be influenced by what you think about. The foundations of your life may be shaky because of a lack of principles that are based on God's word. If you are weakened by the world, you might want to ask yourself some questions. Are my ideas and philosophies of life based on God's word? Am I assured that my decisions in life are reasoned from the Bible? Can I show a verse or concept from scripture that will support my behavior or decisions? If you answer no to the above questions, you will be vulnerable to temptations from the world.

The Devil—The devil works against your flesh because wherever there is an open door, he can have influence. It is possible for the temptation to seem to come out of nowhere. You might find yourself tempted in an area in which you have no sinful pattern. That is truly a temptation of the devil. That is what Jesus experienced. Even though you do not have a sinful stronghold in that area, this temptation can be real. This type of temptation will not be constant, but rather, the devil will look for the best opportunity. When Satan had finished with his temptation against Jesus, he left for a more opportune time (Luke 4:13).

Keys to Victory

Pray—Jesus taught us to pray that we would not be led into temptation but be delivered from evil (Matthew 6:13). When Jesus taught this prayer, it included asking for our daily bread. That would indicate that praying not to be led into temptation is to be done on a regular basis. Pray for God to show you when temptation is approaching. The Holy Spirit is given to you to lead you to full victory.

Watch—We are also told to "watch and pray" that we do not fall into temptation (Matthew 26:41). It requires that we be diligent in our Christian walk. Watch out for temptation before it arrives. Know your battle plan in advance. Which scripture will you use against the temptation? What will you say or do when you are tempted? What environments do you need to avoid? What were hurts or disappointments you were experiencing the last time that temptation came along? Do you know your three greatest weaknesses? Is there a sinful pattern in your life that is opening the door to further temptation?

Grace—Depend on God's help. Ask the Holy Spirit to give you strength. Do not try "willpower," but try dependence upon God. Don't be spiritually proud. It is okay to be weak in yourself, but strong in Christ. Depend on Him and not your ability to overcome.

Don't put yourself into situations where you have fallen in times past. Just say, "I can't go there," and flee. You will find it easier and easier to resist when you do this. As long as you think *you* can handle it, you will be subject to falling into temptation.

Prepare to suffer. When you don't get your way, it will hurt. You are accustomed to doing what you desire. Put forth great resistance, even though God will be helping you. The writer of Hebrews says, "You have not resisted sin to the point of shedding blood" (Hebrews 12:4). This means there is suffering when we turn from sin. Some people have even died for their faith.

He is able to keep you from falling (Jude 1:24). Jesus knows your weakness, and he still loves you. If you do fail, picture God loving you and accepting you while you are in your sin and snared by the tempter. Your victory begins with God's goodness, even though you know you have displeased Him. He remains with you to succor you. Knowing that God still loves you will motivate you to obey Him. God's ability working with you is His grace.

Application

1. What does it mean to be tempted?

that you thinking about going into the
darkness

2. Temptation to sin comes from the _____, the _____, and the _____.

3. James tells us how temptation works.

   1) What comes first? _____

   2) When desire is conceived, it gives birth to _____.

   3) And sin brings forth _____.

4. What scripture tells us that we are not too weak to pass the test of temptation? This Bible verse is one of your memory verses this week. Write it out by memory.

I Cor. 10:13

5. Has God been dealing with you about your environment or influences in your life? Take a moment and submit these to God. Identify the open doors to temptation in each of the areas in which God is dealing.

6. Name the three keys to victory.

   1) _Pray_

   2) _Watch_

   3) _Grace_

Commit to these three keys to victory. Begin now to pray daily for God to keep you from temptations. Practice daily watching for temptations that come your way. Learn where you have been vulnerable. Prepare to suffer when you are tempted. Receive the love, grace, and mercy of God in your steps of victory.

Overcoming Satan

For the past two weeks, you have been learning about the world, sin, and temptation. In each of these lessons, we have referred to the devil and his strategies. This week's lessons are designed to introduce you to the spiritual warfare that you are in, and the means you have been given to overcome your enemy.

There are two extremes when discussing issues related to Satan and demons. First, some think that Satan is not real and that demons do not exist. In our modern world, the idea of the existence of demons may seem primitive and even unenlightened. Science can find physical relationships to most problems; as a result, many people assume that none are related to demonic activity. If one takes this approach, it will lead to not acting in faith against the enemy. The second extreme is to associate most every conflict or problem directly with demons or the devil. To err on this side gives too much credit to the devil and creates curiosity and interest in darkness. This thought pattern can prevent us from seeing our flesh. This error arises from a misunderstanding of Satan's activities and how he operates with his demonic forces. This week we will address how to walk out our victory over our adversary.

Who Is Satan?

The first time we see a reference to the devil is in the Garden of Eden. Here Satan is referred to as "the serpent" (Genesis 3:1). Later, however, the name Satan is given to him in the book of Job; here we read:

> *One day the angels came to present themselves before the LORD, and Satan also came with them. The LORD said to Satan, "Where have you come from?" Satan answered the LORD, "From roaming through the earth and going back and forth in it." (Job 1:6, 7)*

Satan is the Hebrew word for adversary or opponent. Several times in the Old Testament he is referred to as opposing or accusing God's people (Job 1:7; 2:7; 1 Chronicles 21:1; Zechariah 3:1). In the New Testament, we see many names given to him as the leader of the dark forces or fallen angels.

- The devil (Matthew 4:1)

- The ruler of this world (John 12:31; 14:30)

- The prince of the power of the air (Ephesians 2:2)

- The evil one (Matthew 16:11)

- Satan (Matthew 16:23)

- The serpent (2 Corinthians 11:3)

- The tempter (Matthew 4:3; 1 Thessalonians 3:5)

- The accuser (Revelation 12:10)

- Be-elzebul (dung-god) (Matthew 10:25; 12:24)

All of these names reflect some portion of his activities. He is called the tempter not only because of his original temptation of Eve and the temptation of Christ, but he still operates that way against God's people. He is known as the accuser of Christians because he attempts to condemn and tear down what Christ's grace has built in your life. Satan's goal is to get you to turn from God to hinder your progress. This is done through lies, murder, persecution, deception, confusion, or all manner of sin in which he can involve you. Satan will at times bring physical calamity, as in the life of Job, to attempt to turn God's people away from the truth. He will try every scheme to accomplish his goal. His nature and character are described in the Scriptures as the original murderer, liar, and sinner.

He was a murderer from the beginning, not holding to the truth, for there is no truth in him. When he lies, he speaks his native language, for he is a liar and the father of lies. (John 8:44)

. . .the devil has been sinning from the beginning. (I John 3:8)

Satan's Limited Power

God has limited Satan and his demons in their ability and authority. When Jesus went to the cross, He defeated Satan and took all of his authority. Now Satan is only able to operate in the realm of darkness. That is why he is called the "ruler of darkness" (Ephesians 6:12). This limits his means of operation. That is why he must work through deception and temptation. To get a hold on you, he must bring you into sinful patterns or doubt and unbelief. This is his only hope to combat God's work in your life.

Satan's ability is real, but it is restricted. Even in the Old Testament, God limited Satan's ability. When Moses went before Pharaoh's court, through God's power, he performed several miraculous feats. On three different occasions, Pharaoh called for his sorcerers and soothsayers to perform the same acts that Moses had done by God's power. They were able to duplicate three of these acts. When Aaron's rod became a serpent, Pharaoh's soothsayers threw down their staffs, and their staffs became serpents as well. They were able to turn water into blood and brought forth frogs upon the land just like God's miracles through Moses and Aaron. However, in the fourth miracle when Aaron stretched out his rod and lice came forth upon all of Egypt, they tried the same feat with their secret arts but could not (Exodus 7:11, 22; 8:6, 18). They found their power limited and finally acknowledged God.

In the story of Job, God limited Satan's actions in what he could do to Job. He had to ask for permission to do anything to Job. What Satan was not permitted to do, he could not do (Job 1:12; 2:6).

Satan is capable of performing certain mystical acts to entice those who are spiritually hungry. He has done this through false religions and practices of witchcraft and sorcery. That is why many people are deceived into following him. The Bible warns us to stay away from sorcery, witchcraft, interpretation of omens, mediums and spiritualists (Deuteronomy 18:10-12).

God has always limited Satan, but Christ's death dissolved the deeds of the devil and gave individual believers the power over Satan and his demons (1 John 3:8; Hebrews 2:14). Any authority that Satan had over man was lost when Jesus, as a man (the last Adam), defeated Satan and overcame him through His life, death, and resurrection. Paul tells us, "And having disarmed the powers and authorities, he made a public spectacle of them, triumphing over them by the cross" (Colossians 2:15).

Before He went to the cross, Jesus showed His disciples the type of authority He had given to them. He sent them out to heal the sick and tell of the kingdom of God. They returned announcing that even the demons were subject to them. Jesus declared, "I have given you the authority to trample on snakes and scorpions and to overcome all the power of the enemy; nothing will harm you" (Luke 10:19).

Jesus explained His superior power was through the Spirit of God.

> But if I drive out demons by the Spirit of God, then the kingdom of God has come upon you. Or again, how can anyone enter a strong man's house and carry off his possessions unless he first ties up the strong man? Then he can rob his house. (Matthew 12:28, 29)

Jesus bound Satan at the cross. That means Satan was legally defeated and stripped of his authority; however, he is not prevented from operating through deception. This is Satan's mode of operation until he is cast into the lake of fire at the end of history (Revelation 20:10). That is why these lessons are so crucial to you as a disciple to learn to overcome the devil. Christ has won the victory legally and authoritatively, and now you are called to follow his example because He has given you His authority and the power of the Holy Spirit.

Application

1. What two extremes should we guard against when discussing Satan and his demons?

   Satan is not real
   demons don't exist

2. What does the name Satan mean?

   adversary   fallen angel

3. Give at least four names and scripture references for Satan from the New Testament.

4. God has limited Satan and his demons in their _Ability_ and _Authority_.

5. Read Hebrews 2:14. If you have access to different translations of the Bible, try reading it from another version. Rewrite the verse in your own words.

6. Satan as a "strongman" had you in bondage, but Jesus came and set you free. Jesus is the "stronger man" spoken about in Matthew 12:28, 29. What did Jesus do to Satan at the cross?

7. Don't forget to be memorizing this week's memory verses. Turn to the appendix and begin working on this week's first verse.

Demon Forces

In today's lesson, we want to identify demonic powers to understand the struggle that we encounter against Satan and his forces. Since Satan is a spiritual being, he seeks humans through which to work. A demon does not have a human body, so it seeks influence in a body to have a means of expression. That is why Satan and his demons look for areas of influence.

We see examples of this in the New Testament. There was a man demonized by so many demons they called themselves Legion. The man was driven by the demons. He tore his clothes off, had super strength, cut himself with stones, and lived among the tombs and hills. When Jesus set the man free, the demons begged to go into the swine nearby seeking a lower form of a bodily expression. Jesus allowed them to enter the swine and the swine ran into the sea and drowned (Mark 5:1-16).

From the very beginning, Satan has worked to influence humans to oppose God's plans and purposes. As previously stated, that is his primary objective. This influence upon humans can be at different degrees. Those who live in darkness are subject to great sway by demons because they follow the course of the world and the prince of the air, which is Satan.

What about Christians? What kind of influence do demons have on Christians? First of all, since we belong to God and are born of God, the evil one cannot touch us (1 John 5:18). That means Satan has no legal right to us. However, when sinful patterns are present, you have opened the door to Satan. Paul gives us some understanding of this aspect of spiritual warfare. For example, he warns us not to hold on to anger when he writes, "In your anger do not sin: Do not let the sun go down while you are still angry, and do not give the devil a foothold" (Ephesians 4:26, 27).

This is true with any willful sin from which we refuse to turn away. It gives a foothold to the devil. Second, even without a "foothold," the devil will attempt to influence you through lies and deceptions. When Satan tries to influence you in any way, it should be considered an attack.

Satan is not omnipresent. He cannot be in two places at one time, much less be everywhere at once. That is what Paul means when he said we struggle against "the rulers, against the authorities, against the powers of this dark world, and against the spiritual forces of evil in the heavenly realms" (Ephesians 6:12). He is speaking of various levels of demonic powers that have been assigned responsibilities from Satan. The terms he uses here refer to demons that have first place jurisdiction, and wicked spirits with powers of the darkness. That means demons carry out the desires and commands of Satan. Therefore, when the Bible speaks of resisting the devil, it includes the demons that assist him.

Identifying Evil Spirits

It is common for Christians who believe we are in a spiritual battle, to determine many behaviors or symptoms, as the name for that evil spirit. For example, if someone is worrying a lot, they might want to cast out a "spirit of worry." If someone is in unbelief, they might pray against a "spirit of unbelief." Every adverse behavior becomes the name for a demon. Though it is not wrong, per se, to call these behaviors a spirit, it is more scriptural to follow the biblical names and use the authority of God's Word to identify them. For instance, the Bible speaks of a "lying spirit" (1 Kings 22:21, 22). The lying spirit could talk to a person and influence them to worry or be in unbelief. By understanding that, you will sense a greater degree of faith when praying against such. It seems correct to use the biblical names where they are appropriate. It is not necessary to identify every spirit, but when we talk about spiritual warfare, it helps to know the true characteristics of such demons and how God's Word identifies them.

Not every time the word "spirit" is used does it refer to a demon. Sometimes it is used to describe a disposition.[5] A good example of Scripture is what some would call a "spirit of haughtiness." In context it refers to a proud human spirit, not a demon: "Pride goes before destruction, a haughty spirit before a fall" (Proverbs 16:18).

That is not to say that an evil spirit could not tempt someone to pride, but there is no biblical name for such. Other times the word spirit is used to give a contrast to explain the nature of the Holy Spirit. An example of this would be when Paul said that we have not been given a "spirit of fear," but of power and of love and a sound mind (2 Timothy 1:7). He is not saying, "We have not been given a 'demon of fear,' but a Holy Spirit of power." No, he is explaining that timidity is not a characteristic of the Holy Spirit.[6]

General names given to demons identify their character as being evil spirits, unclean spirits, and perverse spirits. These are not specific names but would certainly describe demons of all kinds. However, the Bible does identify at least six evil spirits by name. When applying Christ's authority over the enemy, it may give you clarity in faith and prayer to use the biblical names for these six root spirits.

Biblical Names of Demons

1) Spirit of Infirmity (Luke 13:11-16)—Not every sickness is caused by a demon, but we see from these verses that it is real. The Bible tells us that Jesus went about doing good and healing all that were under the power of the devil (Acts 10:38). A spirit of infirmity may cause chronic illnesses or lingering disorders of the body.

2) Spirit of Divination (Acts 16:16-18)—The spirit of divination was able to predict the future, that is, as far as the people were concerned. Only God knows the future. However, evil spirits may observe people's lives, their talk, and their plans, and communicate to someone with a spirit of divination, thus

---

5 This is true with the "spirit of heaviness," (Isa 61:3); "spirit of stupor," (Rom 11:8); "spirit of jealousy" (Num 5:14).
6 This contrast is also used of "spirit of bondage" (Rom 8:15).

appearing to tell the future. God warns us about having anything to do with witchcraft, mediums, sorcerers, contacting the dead, and the like (Deuteronomy 18:10-12). The Bible says that rebellion is as the sin of witchcraft, so rebellion, stubbornness, and control can be a manifestation of this spirit as well.

3) **Deaf and Mute Spirit** (Mark 9:25-27)—This spirit not only kept a boy from hearing and talking, but it also tried to kill him in water and fire. It apparently threw the boy into convulsions from time to time, including the moment Jesus commanded the spirit to leave. Jesus rebuked the deaf and mute spirit.

4) **Spirit of Whoredoms** [prostitution] (Hosea 4:12)—A spirit that primarily works in the areas of sexual sin and unfaithfulness. It is prevalent in all manner of sexual sin and perverseness, including molestation, rape, incest, lust, seduction, exhibitionism, etc. This demon, like other spirits, looks for influence through sinful patterns.

5) **Lying Spirit** (2 Chronicles 18:22; 1 Kings 22:21, 22)—This spirit works in many areas because the nature of Satan himself is deception and lying. A lying spirit can be traced to rejection, fear, oppression, deception, pride, and many other strongholds.

6) **Spirit of Antichrist** (1 John 4:3)—This spirit works to reject Jesus as the Son of God and brings persecution against the saints and the work of the church. It opposes the miraculous works of Christ. John and the other apostles, no doubt, dealt with this spirit regularly.

Identifying specific names given to evil spirits helps us in our fight against these powers. Tomorrow we will begin dealing with our struggle and how to participate in this spiritual battle.

Colossians 2:14 say to Jesus repentance

Blotting out the hand writing of the ordinances that was set against us, which was contary to us & took it out of the way nailing it the cross

Application

1. What scripture tells us that if we are born of God the evil one does not touch us? Write out the verse.

_____

_____

_____

2. What verse tells us not to give a "foothold" to the devil? Write that verse out as well.

Ephesians 4 26-27 _____

_____

_____

3. Give an example of the word "spirit" referring to the disposition of a human spirit.

_____

_____

_____

4. Give an example of the word "spirit" given to show the contrast and characteristics of the Holy Spirit.

_____

_____

_____

5. Write in the biblical name for the evil spirit described.

infirmity _____ A spirit that primarily works in the areas of sexual sin and unfaithfulness.

divination _____ This spirit brings persecution against the saints.

death spirit _____ Rebellion and control can be symptoms of this spirit.

whoredoms _____ Rejection, fear, oppression, deception, pride, and many other strongholds can often be traced to this spirit.

lying spirit _____ This spirit tried to kill a boy by throwing him in water and fire.

antichrist _____ Chronic illnesses or lingering disorders of the body may be caused by this spirit.

Spiritual Warfare

The Christian life has many facets. While it is a life of joy, peace, and comfort to your soul, you will soon discover that you have an enemy also attacking your soul. You are in a fight. It is called war. It is a fight over your faith. This is not optional. When you became a Christian, you were delivered from the dominion of Satan, and the battle began. Denial or ignorance does not change the reality of the struggle. You are in a war against spiritual forces.

Paul said that we are not fighting against people but spiritual forces. He wrote, "For our struggle is not against flesh and blood, but against the rulers, against the authorities, against the powers of this dark world and against the spiritual forces of evil in the heavenly realms" (Ephesians 6:12).

There are a couple of truths that you should keep in mind when speaking of spiritual warfare. Number one: God is not fighting the devil. He never has. He is God, and the devil is a created being. The devil fights or opposes God, and God's angels fight Satan's wicked forces (Daniel 10:11, 12; Revelation 12:7-9), but God's throne or authority is settled forever in heaven. This spiritual fight is ours to win with the victory that Christ has already accomplished. It brings glory to God when we live out His victory over the world, sin, and the devil.

Number two: everything that is hard is not bad, it is just hard. When hardships or disappointments come, some people blame the devil. Not everything unpleasant is demonic. You can't solve every problem by casting out demons. We must have spiritual discernment and know God's word. Through God's Word, the Bible, and the help of the Holy Spirit we can discern these attacks from life's difficulties.

How Demons Operate

Demons work at all levels of influence. It always begins with the individual and his or her influence. Satan wants to bring destruction to individuals and families. If he can influence the authorities in the home, he has a greater chance to bring forth destructive fruit in a family. His ultimate desire against a family is to bring about generational iniquities. It works the same way with organizations, governments, and churches. The more influence a person has, the more Satan will attempt to bring that person under his control. That is why you will see corruption in high levels of government. Satan wants all the influence he can get.

Church leaders become a specific target for Satan and his demons. The more responsibility that a person receives in the kingdom of God, the greater the target he or she becomes. Satan hates a humble leader. God gives grace to the humble but resists the proud (James 4:6). Pride is how Satan fell. That is why Paul gives Timothy the instruction about an elder, "He must not be a recent convert, or he may become conceited and fall under the same judgment as the devil" (1 Timothy 3:6).

A church leader or responsible Christian should not be fearful but certainly alert. You have a true enemy just waiting for you to give in to darkness. Peter, an apostle and also an elder, warned church leaders, "Be self-controlled and alert. Your enemy the devil prowls around like a roaring lion looking for someone to devour" (1 Peter 5:8).

Ways Demons Influence Christians

1. **Influence your thoughts**—Though demons cannot read your mind, they can place thoughts in your mind. Just as the serpent questioned Eve about what God had said, demons will often try to get you to distrust God. If a demon speaks, it is to your mind or in the spiritual realm.

2. **Influence your heart**—Of course, if a demon speaks to you, the purpose is to influence your will and to get you to change your heart.

   There was a Christian couple in the New Testament church in Jerusalem who lied to the Holy Spirit and Peter. They were trying to appear more generous in their giving than they were. Peter confronted them and said, "How is it that Satan has so filled your heart that you have lied to the Holy Spirit . . ." (Acts 5:3).

   The Bible says that King David was persuaded by Satan to trust in his armies rather than God (1 Chronicles 21:1). Demons can be very seducing. Paul warns believers concerning those who will abandon the faith and follow deceiving spirits (1 Timothy 4:1).

   When Jesus explained to His disciples that He must suffer and die, Peter rejected such thoughts and pulled Jesus aside to tell him that would never happen. Jesus' response was direct: "Get behind me, Satan!" (Matthew 16:23). Peter was saying the things of men rather than the things of God, Jesus knew it was an attempt of Satan to get Him off the path of the Father's will.

   Words of self-pity and self-preservation must be guarded against in spiritual warfare. Demons often come and tell Christians what they want to hear. That is why we must test every spirit (1 John 4:1). The Word of God is our final authority. What you hear spiritually must be judged by the Scripture. That is how Jesus overcame the devil in His time of temptation.

3. **Influence your circumstances**—Some people identify every hardship as being caused by the devil. If they have a flat tire on their way to church, they assume the devil did it. Unless the Holy Spirit reveals it, you should guard against blaming too many circumstances on the devil. You may end up giving him credit for more involvement than he has. Satan is more interested in your response to circumstances. You must guard your heart.

There are times when Satan does directly attempt to hinder. We see this through the persecution brought against Paul that hindered him from going to see the Thessalonians. He wrote to them, "For we wanted to come to you —certainly I, Paul, did, again and again—but Satan stopped us" (1 Thessalonians 2:18).

Jesus came upon a lady bent over and could not straighten up. A spirit of infirmity or sickness had caused this. She had been bound for eighteen years with this illness. This was a daughter of the covenant of Abraham. Jesus said she ought to be released from her infirmity. He set her free from a "spirit of infirmity." Not all sickness is directly caused by demons; however, this account proves that sometimes it is a direct assault upon those in covenant with God (Luke 13:11-16).

Once you identify the operations of Satan, you can exercise your authority in various means of spiritual warfare. Becoming aware of the spiritual battle that you are in will enable you to be alert to the schemes of the devil. That is why we will address various means of spiritual warfare in our upcoming lessons.

Application

1. Paul tells us that we are in a fight. It is not optional; it comes with being a Christian. Write out the verse that tells us this truth.

1st Peter 5:8 ~~the devil~~ your enemy walks around ~~Prowling around~~ like a roaring lion seeking who he can devour

2. There are two truths that should be considered with talking about demons and spiritual warfare. What are they?

your thoughts and your heart

3. Why do you think Satan targets leaders?

Bigger the influence / more people

4. What Scripture tells us why Satan fell? Write it out.

5. Name three ways in which demons attempt to influence Christians. Give an example of each.

6. Ask the Holy Spirit to show you where there have been demonic attacks against you or your family.

Various Means of Warfare

Let's take a look at the various means of spiritual warfare. First of all, when you understand that your Christian life is a spiritual battle, you will be able to recognize that there are many aspects to defeating the enemy. Even choices and decisions that we make can have a tremendous influence on our victories. Spiritual warfare has both a practical and spiritual element. The practical aspects can also be called spiritual because they include decisions and actions taken that represent godliness. These godly decisions close the door to the enemy's plans. The spiritual or mystical[7] aspects of this fight include prayer, commands, and exercising our spiritual authority over the devil. In this lesson, we will address both aspects of practical and spiritual means of warfare.

Practical Means of Spiritual Warfare

There are practical means of spiritual warfare in the life of the Christian. Prayer and rebuking the devil are often seen as the primary means of spiritual warfare, but some practical means must be in place in your life. These areas of spiritual warfare are foundational to a walk of freedom.

1. **Repentance** (Ephesians 4:27)—As we have already emphasized, repentance closes the door to the enemy. Jesus said that the prince of this world had no hold on Him (John 14:30). Since no sin was in Jesus' life, the devil could not get a handle on Him. When you submit to God in repentance, you are participating in a practical means of spiritual warfare. When we tolerate habitual sinful patterns in our life, we are giving in to spiritual warfare. You cannot expect victory over demons if you are holding onto revealed sin in a particular area of your life. When you turn from these areas, you remove a handle from your life. Satan no longer has a means to influence your thoughts and actions.

2. **Obedience** (James 4:7)—Obedience is a part of submitting to God. When you submit yourself to God, you are in a position to resist the enemy of your soul. You cannot have victory over the enemy without first coming before God in true submission. If you try to resist the devil without first coming to God, you will be struggling in your strength. Spiritual warfare includes obedience to God and His authorities (Titus 3:1-5; Romans 13:1-7; Hebrews 3:17). If you operate in rebellion, it will open the door to a spirit of divination because rebellion is as the sin of divination (1 Samuel 15:23). You are now a child of God and should not be participating in "the spirit of darkness that

---

7 The word *mystical* suggests a spiritual meaning or reality that is neither apparent to the senses nor obvious to the intellect. It is used here to refer to the supernatural or spiritual aspects, not mystical as in witchcraft.

works in the children of disobedience" (Ephesians 2:2). Submission and obedience have power against darkness since Satan operates in rebellion against God.

3. **Forgiveness** (Matthew 18:21-35)—A very vital means of spiritual warfare is forgiveness. It involves several areas of spiritual warfare. It includes submission to God, repentance, obedience, and faith. It takes trust in God to release someone through forgiveness. Keeping anger in your heart, even overnight, gives a foothold to the devil (Ephesians 4:26). The word for devil can be translated *slanderer*, and that is just what happens. You come under the legal attack of the enemy when you hold anger in your heart. Unresolved anger quickly grows into unforgiveness, which produces a root of bitterness. Once bitterness enters your life other aspects of your life become defiled (Hebrews 12:15). A root of bitterness can bear the fruit of rage, hatred, resentment, and control. Fruit of bitterness can even lead to the self-indulgence of addictions, depression, and despondency.

    Jesus included this dynamic aspect in the prayer that He taught the disciples, "Forgive us our sins as we forgive those who have sinned against us" Matthew 6:12). Jesus also taught in a parable that if we do not forgive we will be turned over to tormentors (Matthew 18:21-35).

4. **Giving** (2 Corinthians 8-9)—Giving may seem more like a spiritual discipline than a means of spiritual warfare; however, I have listed it because of three major counterattacks that giving produces. First, giving produces mission-centeredness for the kingdom. The grace of God compels Christians to give (2 Corinthians 8:1-5). The foundation of the great commission is in giving. It leads you to keep your focus on God's will. Second, giving breaks the stronghold of greed and selfishness (Luke 12:13-21). Giving works as an antidote to this stronghold. Giving also manifests the plenteousness of God, which helps guard against fear, worry, doubt, and unbelief. It is God who provides the material things so that you have something to give (2 Corinthians 9:8-14), thus trust in God frees us from fear. Since giving operates in the opposite disposition of greed, selfishness, covetousness, and fear, it can be called spiritual warfare.

5. **Resistance** (James 4:7)—Resisting the devil and evil is a vital part of spiritual warfare. It is always spiritually profitable to resist the devil and run from evil. When you are submitted to God, you can resist the devil. This is called standing and walking by faith. We resist by standing in our evil day. The evil day is the day when our strongest temptations come. Resistance includes fleeing lust and temptation (1 Corinthians 6:18; 2 Timothy 2:22; 1 Timothy 6:11). It requires the fear of the Lord, and a wise man, to depart from evil (Proverbs 14:16; 16:6). Peter tells elders to resist their adversary the devil steadfastly in faith. This requires standing strong in spite of what you see or feel.

Spiritual Means of Warfare

There are spiritual means to carry out warfare against demons and darkness.

1. **Prayer** (Ephesians 6:18)—Prayer can be considered one of the most important means of spiritual warfare. As Daniel the prophet prayed and fasted for God's revelation for the people of Israel, the

angels came on his behalf. A demonic force called "the prince of Persia," a ruling spirit over that nation prevented Gabriel from getting to Daniel. Gabriel told Daniel that the angels came from the first day he set himself to pray and that Michael, one of the chief angels, came to help defend Gabriel to get the message to Daniel (Daniel 10:1-15). When we pray, God may send angels to act on our behalf as ministering spirits (Hebrews 1:14). We are instructed to pray always with all prayer in the spirit in our battle against principalities and powers (Ephesians 6:10-18).

2. **Fasting** (Matthew 17:14-21)—Jesus indicates that fasting and prayer work together in deliverance. It helps us to focus on God's Word for faith to operate. Jesus said that some spirits do not go out except by prayer and fasting. Fasting helps to deal with our unbelief. Turning away from our flesh opens our hearts to hear the word of God. Thus faith comes (Romans 10:17).

3. **Faith** (Ephesians 6:16)—Faith and prayer could be seen as equally important. Faith is the very essence of our fight, for Paul called it a fight of faith (1 Timothy 6:12). Jesus told Peter that Satan had asked to test him, and Jesus prayed that his faith would not fail (Luke 22:31, 32). To hold fast to what God has said is spiritual warfare. Faith resists the lies of the enemy. This was the very test that Eve failed in the Garden.

4. **Praise and Worship** (Psalm 149; 95:6)—The very nature of worship is a powerful weapon in spiritual warfare. In humility of worship, one must listen, receive instruction, and obey. While we worship, God acts on our behalf (2 Chronicles 20:22). Praise is often defined with declarations, shouts of joy, processions, clapping of hands, singing, and dancing. These all signify a strong confidence in God's ability to bring deliverance.

While several of these means could be considered spiritual disciplines, such as prayer, fasting, giving, as well as praise and worship, they also serve as means of warfare. The above-mentioned means represent the armor of God or the defensive means of warfare. In our next lesson, we will address the offensive aspects of warfare.

6:30   snacks
Bible study
4-8-21

Application

1. Spiritual warfare has both a _practical_ and _spiritual_ element.

2. Take the five practical means of spiritual warfare and give a short explanation of why each is important.

    1) Repentance _Collians 3:23_ _____

    _____

    2) Obedience _____

    _____

    3) Forgiveness _____

    _____

    4) Giving _____

    _____

    5) Resistance _____

    _____

3. What Old Testament reference do we have that teaches that God sends angels to fight on behalf of prayer?

    _____

    _____

    _____

4. Jesus said that some spirits do not come out except by prayer and _____.

5. The very essence of spiritual warfare is a fight of _____.

6. Work on your second memory verse for the week. Be prepared to quote your verses in class if called upon.

Exercising Authority in Warfare

In the life of Jesus, demons often cried out when He came close to them. They recognized His authority and often manifested in His presence. Apparently, these demons were not comfortable to remain in His presence without crying out and attempting to flee. This may not have happened each time, but we have several references to this occurring. When Jesus was teaching in the synagogue in Capernaum, an evil spirit cried out, "What do you want with us, Jesus of Nazareth? Have you come to destroy us? I know who you are—the Holy One of God!" A man in the audience stood up and shouted these words with his own voice even though they came from the evil spirits. Another account of such manifestations took place when Jesus approached the man in the country of Gerasenes. This man was filled with so many demons they identified themselves as "Legion, for we are many" (Mark 5:9).

> *When he saw Jesus from a distance, he ran and fell on his knees in front of him. He shouted at the top of his voice, "What do you want with me, Jesus, Son of the Most High God? Swear to God that you won't torture me!"* (Mark 5:6, 7)

These demons were very much aware of who Jesus was and when He was in their presence. Jesus drove out demons by the power of the Holy Spirit, but it was Christ's authority and His name the demons feared.

When Jesus gave this authority to His disciples, it was not only transferred to them, but after Pentecost, it was given to all who believed. Membership in God's family provides you the same legal authority to cast out demons. Jesus said that signs would follow those who believe and in His name they would cast out demons (Mark 16:17). However, Jesus' authority is only given to Christians. We are given an account of Jews who tried to use Jesus' name without His authority. We see this event in the Book of Acts;

> *A team of itinerant Jews who was traveling from town to town casting out demons planned to experiment by using the name of the Lord Jesus. The incantation they decided on was this: "I adjure you by Jesus, whom Paul preaches, to come out!" Seven sons of Sceva, a Jewish priest, were doing this. But when they tried it on a man possessed by a demon, the demon replied, "I know Jesus and I know Paul, but who are you?" And he leaped on two of them and beat them up, so that they fled out of his house naked and badly injured.* (Acts 19:13-16)

Exercising Authority Through Commands

In the New Testament, we have examples of spirits being cast out and commanded to leave individuals. Paul used this means when he commanded the spirit of divination to leave a soothsaying girl. She followed him and his workers around for many days saying good things. She kept declaring that Paul and these men were from God and were telling people the way of salvation. On the surface, this was fine, but the Holy Spirit revealed to Paul that she spoke by an evil spirit. Luke, one of Paul's workers, writes, "Finally Paul became so troubled that he turned around and said to the spirit, 'In the name of Jesus Christ I command you to come out of her!' At that moment the spirit left her" (Acts 16:18).

While it is appropriate to pray against demons, there are times when a command is appropriate. In the same way that God has chosen people to preach the gospel, He has decided to give us the authority to command demons to leave. You may pray for someone to be encouraged, but you are still expected to speak words of encouragement. God has given us a vital responsibility to participate with Him in using our voice in commanding evil spirits to depart.

To rebuke an unclean spirit does not require a loud volume or excessive emotionally charged rebuke, but a firm faith-filled command. A brief command speaking directly to the spirit to leave and not return is sufficient. You need not be afraid of demons. The power of the Holy Spirit and the authority of Jesus are more than adequate to bring about deliverance.

Commanding evil spirits to leave need not frighten the one who is receiving the ministry. Wayne Grudem writes, "It is often considerate simply to ask questions of the person we are helping. We might ask, 'Do you think an evil spirit may be attacking you in this situation?' or 'Would you mind if I spoke a word of rebuke to an evil spirit that may be a factor in this?'"[8]

If it is not appropriate to command the spirit aloud at that moment, it can be done in private prayer. The command should be spoken audibly, however, because we have no indication that demons can read our minds. Simply say, "I command that lying spirit (or whatever spirit you have identified) to leave and not return." Then pray for God's blessings upon that person.

Exercising Authority Through the Word

The Bible tells us our offensive weapon is the sword of the Spirit which is the Word of God (Ephesians 6:17). Jesus demonstrated its power against the devil when He was tempted in the wilderness. Each time He was tempted, He quoted the Scriptures and said, "It is written!" (Luke 4:1-13).

Simple attacks are often overcome by daily devotional time with God and hearing the Word of God. There are times, no doubt, that spirits have departed when one is sitting under anointed preaching and prayer. The power of God is in the Gospel. More severe strongholds, however, may take other measures. Any time deliverance is brought to a person they must be filled with the Word of God afterward. The daily application of the Word is a guard against deception and a snare.

When Paul spoke of his authority to confront false apostles and false teaching, he was talking about the Word that he preached. He declared that the weapons of his warfare were not of this world, but mighty

---

8 Wayne Grudem, *Systematic Theology, An Introduction to Biblical Doctrine* (Grand Rapids, MI: Zondervan Publishing House, 1994), 431.

through God. He said that he would tear down strongholds that were built up against the knowledge of God (2 Corinthians 10:4, 5). The Word of God is one of our main offensive weapons.

Exercising Authority Through Prayer

Though we have already mentioned prayer earlier, it must be reiterated as a powerful weapon to be exercised against the works of darkness. We should pray in the spirit and pray specifically. When the Holy Spirit reveals an area of bondage, that is the time to identify its nature and pray expressly against the actions of that spirit. Paul tells us to pray with all kinds of prayer without ceasing. Faith and prayer work together, blocking the fiery darts of the enemy.

Exercising Authority Through Actions

Whatever you see prevailing from the kingdom of darkness, you can counter by living and acting in the opposite spirit. If perversion is prevalent, then the Christian should manifest purity. The Church is to be the salt and light to the world. Your life stands in contrast to darkness. When proper actions and decisions are kept, the influence of demonic power is broken. Each believer who acts in the opposite spirit diminishes Satan's strongholds. As believers, we live in the light of Christ, and there is no darkness in Him (1 John 1:5).

Be bold and be strong in your spiritual journey. Take this lesson to heart and apply it to your life. Confidence in Christ's authority that he has given to you will rise in your heart as you practice spiritual warfare. Remember, every day you are in a battle. You do not need to be alarmed at all. Just be alert. Fight the good fight.

Application

1. What did evil spirits often do in the presence of Jesus?

   they bowed down or flee

2. Read Mark 16:17. Jesus tells us that signs will follow them that believe. What sign should follow believers concerning demons?

3. What was the soothsaying girl saying about Paul and those working with him?

4. After many days, Paul turned to the girl and said. . . (Write out Paul's command.)

5. While it is appropriate to pray against demons, there are times when a _____ is necessary.

6. To rebuke an unclean spirit does not require loud volume or an excessive, emotionally-charged rebuke, but a firm _____-_____ command.

7. What does the Bible call the sword of the Spirit?

8. Read Ephesians 6:18. Rewrite the verse in your own words.

9. We should act in the _____ _____ when confronting forces of darkness.

Week Four – Day One

Overcoming Your Past

By now it should be clear in your mind that Christ has paid the full price for your sins and that your past is not held against you. If that is the case, why do so many people struggle with what has taken place in their lives before they became Christians or even since? A person's past struggles may include things he has done, spoken, or trauma that has been committed against him or her. In this week's lessons, we will address the need and means to overcome your past.

Proper Perspective of the Past

With past rejections, some people find it difficult to truly believe that God presently loves them fully. It is easy for them to believe that God loves others. This person may have a strong love for God, but it is hard for him to receive the Father's love for himself. When someone has trouble receiving His love, he also struggles with forgiveness from the past. This individual will often say, "I know God forgives me, but I just can't forgive myself." It is true, he has a mental knowledge that God is willing and has forgiven him, but he does not have an experiential knowledge of His love and forgiveness. Once a person has truly been embraced by the Father's love and has received a working revelation of His grace, that is all that matters. When you have received the revelation of God's forgiveness, you will know that you do not have the right to go and dredge up anything that God has forgiven and removed (Psalm 103:12; Isaiah 38:17).

Past experiences can stand as a block to receiving the heavenly Father's love. This can be tied to an individual's perception of love from earthly parents, particularly a father. Since we are born with the sinful nature, it is possible for you to have grown up in a loving environment, but still feel isolated and unloved. Never forget, the devil is the father of all lies. You could have been told all your life that you were unfit and unlovable by Satan himself. You can have feelings of rejection without having abusive or disengaged parents. It is possible for parents to have communicated their love, but because of rebellion or sin in the life of the child, that child will experience similar feelings of isolation. Remember, perception is truth to the person who is experiencing the trauma.

All families are dysfunctional to some degree. Since all have sinned and come short of God's glory, the perfect home does not exist. Even in the best of families, unfortunate events will happen that bring hurts and wounds. In truth, most parents did the best job they could with the knowledge and skills they possessed. They too were often victims of their past. Since these areas don't get addressed, they are passed on to the next generation. Parents often repeat how they were parented.

With our need to identify events from the past in these upcoming lessons, it is important not to play the blame game for your present condition. You cannot change what has happened to you by heaping up guilt or revenge on parents or siblings. Your family of origin helps to reveal how and when a situation may have come into your life, but it is not a means to place blame. That will only produce self-pity and further isolate you. That in and of itself will hinder you from receiving the Father's love because ultimately you must deal with the fact that God placed you in the family in which you were born. You must decide if you are going to be a victim or victor concerning your past. While it is appropriate and necessary for the Holy Spirit to shed light on your past, in order to identify traumas or transgressions, you must remember your problem is not with what has happened to you, but rather your response to what happened to you. The reason to examine the past is to apply God's grace, forgiveness, love, and acceptance to those events. It is the process of presenting your entire life to God with nothing hidden.

We have biblical examples of people who encountered very painful and challenging experiences in life, yet it turned for their good. Joseph is just one great example of someone who grew up in a dysfunctional family, yet he fulfilled God's purpose for his life. He had a father who favored him, and thus he suffered sibling rivalry. His mother died while he was young so he must have experienced abandonment. He endured betrayal at the hands of his brothers, yet he was able to see God as sovereign in his circumstances. He gave the proper response to these events when he had to face forgiving his brothers who sold him into slavery. He declared, "You intended to harm me, but God intended it for good to accomplish what is now being done, the saving of many lives" (Genesis 50:20).

Joseph saw how God used these trials and sufferings to bring him to where he needed to be. You must decide which way you will view your life's experiences. Knowing that God has a way to make all things work for the good of those who love him, who have been called according to his purpose (Romans 8:28) you will mature into a stronger person. You can profit from every adversity. When you see God's sovereign work in your life, you will be able to trust Him to bring full healing and victory over your past.

You will also be able to identify with those who are suffering from their past. God often uses such events in a person's life to become the strength of that individual's ministry to others. It has been said, "Your mess becomes your message, and your misery becomes your ministry." When you experience healing, and walk in victory, you demonstrate authority and power in dealing with the same affliction in others. You will have an entrance to speak into their lives.

You must embrace your past to overcome it. Some people believe they can push problems and feelings aside and not deal with them. These problems do not go away but become heavy emotional baggage. Without healing these wounds from the past, a believer will not walk in the fullness of victory. These traumas will bring up emotions and feelings that seem very similar to what they experienced years earlier. They may not make a connection at first, but a regular pattern of behavior and bad relationships occur even years later. These wounds become triggers to emotional pain. It can become an unending cycle of hurts and destruction.

Evidence of the Past

When a person becomes a Christian, the past is forgiven, but there may be evidence of hurt or damaged emotions. These areas need the healing power of God's love and grace. When we discover inner rawness, constant irritability, little or no tolerance for others, or over-sensitivity to others and circumstances, these can show us a need for further healing.

Some common evidence

1. **Deep Sense of Unworthiness.** This produces feelings of inadequacy, inferiority, and anxiety. Sometimes you can see this in a person's posture. Typical remarks—"I'm no good," or, "No one could ever possibly love me."

2. **Super Sensitivity.** This individual will give an inordinate response to normal circumstances. Conflicts are common in relationships. Common remarks—"People are not friendly," or, "People hurt me!"

3. **Persistent Fears.** Fear of failure or not measuring up can be another evidence of the past. Typical remarks—"This is not going to work out," or, "You just don't know what could happen."

4. **Self-Pity.** This is an excessive amount of selfishness that can stem from past hurts. Common remarks—"I care so much, why doesn't he?" or "Why has this happened to me?"

5. **Perfectionists.** This person can never seem to do something well enough. He can be judgmental of other's efforts as well. Common remarks—"Can't anybody do anything right?" or "I can't believe I did that."

6. **Distrust of Authority.** Defiance, stubbornness, and outright rebellion may come from past trauma. Common remarks—"Nobody is going to tell me what to do," or, "I am not anybody's *yes* man."

7. **Harshness.** This person has a hard time seeing when he is mean. Comments that hurt others are seen as normal. Common remarks—"They are just too sensitive," or "Get over it."

8. **Addictions.** Addictions of all kinds—substance and sexual.

Damaged emotions are not necessarily the only reason for the struggles mentioned above; however, one should examine to see where these patterns were present in his family or when they began in his life. It is not uncommon to discover these same behaviors in the family over several generations. Do not embrace these as acceptable in your life, but seek your healing from Christ.

Application

1. Because of past rejections, some people find it difficult to truly believe that God __loves__ them.

2. When someone is struggling to forgive himself or herself, what is it they really need?

   _____

   _____

3. Explain how it is possible for a person to have feelings of rejection even if he grew up in seemingly a good environment.

   _____ It comes down from past generations

   _____

4. How do we know that all families are dysfunctional to some degree?

   _____

   _____

5. If a person suffers from his past, it is important to remember that his problem is not with what happened to them, but . . .

   _____

   _____

6. What was Joseph's response to the betrayal of his brothers?

   _____

   _____

7. There is a list of eight common evidences of lingering past hurts and traumas. Ask the Holy Spirit to reveal to you if you have any of the eight in your life. If you struggle with something from your past that is not listed in one of the eight categories, be sure and write it down as well.

   _____ perfections

   _____

Wounds from the Past

Today's lesson may be challenging for some; nevertheless, that is the reason we must address wounds from the past. With the proper perspective of your past, you will be able to receive the healing that is necessary for your spiritual growth.

Some may ask, "If we are new creations in Christ, why do we need to be healed from our past?" "If all things became new, why is that not taken care of when we come to Jesus?" In truth, it is taken care of in Christ. First of all, legally you have been made a new creation in Christ (2 Corinthians 5:17). Second, many hurts and wounds have been healed in you that you never realized. You may testify to feeling free and light since you turned your life over to Jesus. You may feel the weight of sin lifted off your life. You know you have been healed. No doubt, we are delivered from many seeds of destruction and generational patterns of sin that will never bear fruit. Only God knows from all that he has saved us.

Then, why not all wounds? The answer is the same with habits and vices. Some people find that when they come to Jesus, they are immediately free from many years of drugs, alcoholism, and other bondages, yet they struggle over other sins and habits that hang on mercilessly. Why God delivers us immediately out of some problems and wants us to grow out of others, only remains in His purpose.

He knows His grace is sufficient for you to rule in the victory over those areas that are left. Through this process, you are made strong. God has provided a means of victory for those weights that so easily beset you. We are instructed in the Bible, "Therefore, since we are surrounded by such a great cloud of witnesses, let us throw off everything that hinders and the sin that so easily entangles, and let us run with perseverance the race marked out for us" (Hebrews 12:1).

The purpose of God in your life is to reign with Christ and reveal the glory of God by overcoming Satan, this world, and the flesh. He is working His image in you. What you learn and experience in walking out victories will be much more valuable to you as a Christian. Your ministry to others will not be from your immediate deliverance, but rather, from your struggles and witness of God's power. It is out of these remaining hurts, damaged emotions, and entanglements of sin that you will be able to see God's power demonstrated. Don't see this as moments of defeat, but rather opportunities for God's grace to reveal His strength in your weakness.

Wounds of Rejection

There are other consequences of wounds rather than rejection; however, in more than four decades of ministry, I have discovered that feelings of rejection are the most prominent among those I have counseled. It stands to reason why rejection is a major problem. In sin, we experience a separation and rejection from God. After coming to Christ and being accepted by God, Satan attempts to attack our acceptance through human rejections.

Wounds may come from words, emotional environments, and actions taken by parents, authorities, or others in a person's life. You may not have ever considered those events to have affected you, yet they can form your thinking patterns and how you view yourself, God, and others. Here are some examples:

Words—"I wish you had never been born!" "We would have been better off with fewer children." "We should have stopped having children after our first child." "Everything you touch turns to mud." "Can't you ever do anything right?" "Why are you such a baby?" "I wish we had had a boy/girl." "Are you stupid?" "I think you must be retarded!" "Why can't you be like other children?" "I can never love him/her." These are just a few of the many wounding statements hurting parents have used that brought damage to their children. You may have some that come to mind as you read these. It is amazing how you can remember them.

Emotions—Children can feel when they are not loved or wanted even while they are very young. Studies have confirmed that children in their mother's womb have been affected by emotional trauma or an unwanted pregnancy. Also, other young siblings can pick up these emotions. In Jeff Hensley's book, *The Zero People: Essays on Life*, he confirms these studies and writes, "even younger children know of their mother's early pregnancy, abortion, and miscarriage."[9] Without words spoken, feelings of rejection can come from such traumas. Children interpret life through their emotions in the first few years. The *National Scientific Council on the Developing Child* from Harvard University states, "As young children develop, their early emotional experiences literally become embedded in the architecture of their brans." They cannot reason beyond their emotions, so many concepts of life are formed from the emotions of a child in their early years.

Actions—Parents can bring emotional trauma by confiding in their children about matters that should not be shared. In their desperation, parents have told their children they were considering suicide or leaving. That child's stability is immediately destroyed. A role reversal takes place when children are brought into the parent's world of alcoholism, drugs, or emotional trauma. The child feels responsible for the parent, thus undermining the child's security. Also, divorced parents often fall into this trap of involving their children in adult matters. In their book, *Love is a Choice, Breaking the Cycle of Addictive Relationships*, the authors, call it emotional incest.[10]

Parental conflicts that cause deep strife, divorce, or abandonment serve to wound a young child's sense of worth. Many children feel guilty over the parent's divorce or conflicts. They may blame themselves for their parent's divorce. They may have nagging questions that lead to feelings of abandonment, "Why did my parents not want me?" "Why didn't they love me more than what they were doing?" "Was

---

9 Jeff Lane Hensley, *The Zero People: Essays on Life*, (Charis Books, 1983), 128.
10 Robert Hemfelt, Frank Minirth, *Love is a Choice, The Definitive Book on Letting Go of Unhealthy Relationships* (Nashville, Tenn.: Thomas Nelson, 1989), 50.

something wrong with me that Dad or Mom did not want to be with me?" Emotionally, it is natural for children to blame themselves.

Of course, physically or verbally abusive behavior can create rejection in the mind of children. Children often grow up thinking they deserve that same kind of treatment. If their parents, who are authorities in their lives, are doing this, then in their minds they must deserve it. Believing they deserve the abuse is a child's way of dealing with the abnormal behavior of a parent. In turn, it becomes almost natural for them to become what they see as normal.

Identifying Rejection

By examining the following questions, you may be able to determine if rejection is part of your life. I have added and altered these questions, but most of these come from *Healing the Wounded Spirit* by John and Paula Sandford.

- Are your feelings easily hurt?
- Do you nurse hurt feelings?
- Do you take remarks as personal insults that others would ignore, laugh at, or enjoy?
- Are you persistently defensive?
- Can you receive correction or instruction without taking it personally?
- Do you need a special invitation or encouragement to participate in activities others would simply volunteer to join?
- Do you demand attention rather than invite it?
- Do you withdraw and find it difficult to share with others?
- Do you talk a lot without revealing what you think?
- Do you seek compliments?
- Do you expect to be overlooked?
- Are you prone to jealousy in relationships?
- Do you read between the lines to judge what people think of you?
- Do you put yourself down or brag about what you have done?
- Do you always feel like you are on the outside of what is going on?
- When things are going well, is it difficult for you to enjoy it for fear that it may change any minute?
- Are you hard and judgmental of yourself and others?

In the Application portion of this lesson, allow the Holy Spirit to prepare you for healing. Remember, we are all are being healed in some areas.

Application

1. Your ministry to others will not be from your immediate deliverance, but rather, from your _____ and _____ of God's power.

2. Today's application portion of the lesson is to serve as a ministry tool in your life. Take a look at the examples given concerning statements or words made by parents or authorities that can bring damage to emotions. Select the ones to which you relate, or write out some that come to your mind from your own experiences.

_____

_____

_____

_____

_____

3. Are there emotional traumas or actions that you have experienced that could have left you with wounds of rejection? Take a moment and write them out.

_____

_____

_____

_____

4. Take the questions from the previous page and list the ones that relate to you, if any.

_probally jude otter_____

_____

_____

_____

Self-Inflicted Wounds

In war, there are times when injuries and fatalities occur from friendly fire when soldiers from the same side accidentally fire upon one another. At other times there may be an accidental discharge of weapons or explosives that cause fatalities as well. Each of these events it is entirely unintentional, yet very unfortunate. Well, in spiritual battles there is something that is even worse; that is when individual soldiers in God's army inflict wounds upon themselves. It is not accidental, yet it may be unknown to the person himself. The enemy loves this. What better way to defeat God's people than for there to be self-inflicted wounds and the person not even know? In today's lesson, we want to focus on three ways in which this happens: through vows and judgments, self-talk, and destructive thinking.

Vows and Judgments

To make a vow means that one utters a solemn promise or assertion; specifically: one by which a person is bound to an act, service, or condition. A judgment is a formal utterance of an authoritative opinion.[11] Experiences and perceptions of traumatic events may shape you if you form inner beliefs through vows and judgments. What you say to yourself about what has happened to you, may be worse than the event itself. When an inner vow is made, it can commit you to act in specific ways.

An example of an inner vow could come from a sexual abuse trauma. An example of a young lady making a vow might say in her heart, "I will never let another man touch me." Later in life, she gets married and may find it difficult to give herself to her husband. A judgment out of the same trauma would be similar, except it comes from an uttered authoritative opinion, such as, "You can't trust men!" It is possible for an abused mother to make a similar judgment to her daughter, thus placing a vow or judgment upon herself and her daughter.

Other examples of vows and judgments:

- Growing up in poverty: Vow—"I will never be without." This can cause a person to be driven and never content. Judgment—"You are not important unless you have things."

- Rejection from a lover: Vow—"I will never let that happen to me again." This can cause one to break relationships when they get too serious because of the fear of being rejected. Judgment—"You can't open yourself to love, or you will get hurt."

---

11 Merriam Webster Dictionary

- Authoritative abuse: Vow—"I will never trust or submit to authority again." This can prevent one from submitting to godly leadership. Judgment—"I must hold something back and not join in completely."

- Cheated: Vow—"I will never trust someone like that again." This can create a distance in this person's relationships. Judgment—"You can't trust people."

- Rejected by a parent: Vow—"I will protect myself by not getting too close." This person will build a shell or protection through isolation in his life. Judgment—"I am unlovable."

You can fill in your own blanks of possible vows and judgments, for there are limitless possibilities. If these examples remind you of some that you have made, your spiritual progress will be hindered. These judgments and vows work against you in the same way that bitterness does. Both come from hurt or unresolved trauma. These vows and judgments will come into play with your present relationships and pressures of life. How a husband views his wife, may be in direct relationship to vows or judgments that he has made about women. How a person responds to church leadership, or a boss, may be in proportion to his judgments made about parental authority or even God. And how you respond to life's conflicts and struggles may be in correlation to judgments that you have made.

Self-Talk and Destructive Thoughts

Self-talk is similar to judgments in that it is what you tell yourself about life experiences about yourself. We all have constant inner conversations with ourselves about the events and the world around us. This self-talk determines your outward responses.

Your self-talk can be destructive to yourself.

> *The tongue that brings healing is a tree of life, but a deceitful tongue crushes the spirit.*
> (Proverbs 15:4)

> *The tongue has the power of life and death, and those who love it will eat its fruit.*
> (Proverbs 18:21)

You can say or act one way for a while, but what you think in your heart and what you tell yourself, is the way you are. The Book of Proverbs speaks about going and sitting down to eat with a stingy man. He may be telling you to eat all you want, but inside he is thinking that you should only take a small amount. As he thinks in his heart, that is the way he is (Proverbs 23:7). So it is with us. What you are telling yourself is the way you will respond.

People have mental pictures or images that affect response to life's events. These mental pictures can be destructive thoughts. These thoughts are developed from past experiences and observing those in authority in their life. People who were influential in a person's life, prejudice these. For example, you may deal with a crisis in the same way that you observed your parents dealing with the crisis. It is not uncommon to dislike something about your parents that you see happening in yourself. This has come from an image or picture in your mind. If your parents expressed harsh anger in discipline, that could become your mode of operation with your children.

The more you think about something in your mind, the more it influences you. I am not suggesting that you ignore or suppress thoughts, but you must learn to allow Christ into this area of your life. If you do not take your hurt to Christ and learn to resolve conflict, then you will be building up destructive thoughts that produce resentment and powerfully negative attitudes toward others.

What negative talk do you have in your life? Are you telling yourself that you will never amount to anything? Are you saying, that you do not deserve better? Ask the Holy Spirit to reveal any self-talk or destructive thoughts that may be holding you back from the purposes of God in your life.

Steps to Victory

1. Identify vows, judgments, negative self-talk, or destructive thoughts.

2. Write them out so you can see them before your eyes.

3. Renounce lies about yourself and others and making such vows or judgments.

4. Ask God to release you from your vows and judgments.

5. Invite Jesus to heal you from your past hurts where these vows and judgments have been made.

6. Now say, "Lord, I break these destructive vows that I have made; bring an end to their damaging means and displace them with your love."

7. Tell the Lord that you choose to think on whatever is true, whatever is noble, whatever is right, whatever is pure, whatever is lovely, whatever is admirable—anything excellent or praiseworthy—you will think about such things (Philippians 4:8).

Application

1. To make a vow means that one utters a _Solemn promise assertion_ or assertion; specifically: one by which a person is bound to an _act_ , _service_ or condition.

2. A judgment is a formal utterance of an _authoritative_ opinion.

3. Write out examples of vows or judgments that you can think of that are not mentioned in this lesson.

    Vow

    _____

    _____

    _____

    Judgment

    _____

    _____

    _____

4. What self-talk do you hear yourself repeat? Is it positive or negative?

    postive - No matter what happenes God will turn it around for the good

    _____

5. Write out in your own words one of the verses from Proverbs that tells us of the power of the tongue.

    proverbs 18:21 life And death are in the power of the toungue and they that love it will eat the fryit

6. Turn to your memory verses and meditate upon each of them. Be prepared to share the memory verses in class.

Generational Iniquities

Everyone has heard someone say, "Well, he is just like his dad!" Then they proceed to describe some adverse behavior such as alcoholism, sexual promiscuousness, or fits of rage.

Since Satan rules in the area of darkness, one of his schemes is to see generational iniquities established in a family from unrepentant sin. A generational iniquity speaks of a tendency or propensity for a particular weakness. God said He would visit the iniquity of the fathers upon the third and fourth generation.

> *You shall not worship them or serve them; for I, the LORD your God, am a jealous God, visiting the iniquity of the fathers on the children, and on the third and the fourth {generations} of those who hate Me.* (Deuteronomy 5:9, 10) (NAS)

In this passage, as well as Exodus 20:5, God is speaking of those who hate Him and are involved in the worship of idolatry. However, the pattern is the same for any sin that a person holds onto in his life. To hold onto known sin, and refuse to turn from it, is idolatry. That individual has placed his will and desire above God's. God said He would "visit" the iniquity of the fathers on the children. The New International Version gives an unfortunate translation of the word "punish." The term *visit* accurately translated here in the New American Standard Version, is more appropriate. The Hebrew word in the text is paqad (paw-kad), which means to visit.[12] This same word is often translated: to be counted toward or numbered with. The word for "punish," yacar (yaw-sar), is translated from the Hebrew as to chastise, bind, or punish and is not used here in either of these passages. So, God does not punish, but rather visits the iniquities up to the third and fourth generation, unless Christ's covenant is applied. While there is no guilt from the sins of the fathers passed on to the children, there are tendencies or weaknesses in these areas.

In their book, *Healing the Wounded Spirit*, John and Paula Sanford state,

> "Satan enters to prey upon physical weaknesses, to exploit sinful tendencies, to cause proclivities to become addictions, proneness to accidents to become tragedies, bad examples to become traps, necessities to reap to escalate to whirlwinds of destruction."[13]

---

12 Strongs Hebrew Greek Dictionary
13 John and Paula Sandford, *Healing The Wounded Spirit* (Tulsa, OK: Victory House Inc., 1985), 388.

Biblical Examples of Generational Patterns

We see some biblical examples of generational patterns. Dr. William Berman and Dr. Dale Doty, expound on this subject in their book, *Shaking the Family Tree;*

> *Starting with Abraham, the pattern of deceit shows up in each succeeding generation. For instance, Abraham twice passes Sarah off as his sister (a half-truth) in order to escape being murdered. Isaac, Abraham's son, followed suit and lied about Rebekah being his sister. When Jacob came along he deceived Isaac and stole Esau's birthright and blessing. Then Laban, Jacob's father-in-law, deceived Jacob by giving him Leah in marriage rather than Rachel. Imagine Jacob's surprise when he awoke in the morning with the wrong woman in his bed! Jacob's sons lied to him about Joseph's death, and then Joseph tricked them all into bringing Benjamin to Egypt.[14]*

David was four generations from Rahab, the harlot (Matthew 1:5, 6). David not only gave into this generational pattern of sexual weakness by committing adultery with Bathsheba (2 Samuel 11:3, 4), but his sons also struggled in this area. David's son Solomon ended up marrying 700 wives and 300 concubines, evidence of an uncontrolled desire. Ammon, another son of David, raped his brother's sister, Tamar (2 Samuel 13:1).

How to Detect Generational Patterns

The key to detecting generational iniquities is to look for existing patterns. A generational iniquity may skip a generation. Having immoral behavior in a family does not mean that every child will necessarily fall prey to the weakness. Satan will use these patterns to work with other sin and strongholds that are in the life of an individual, most often stubbornness or rebellion. Remember, God's warning was for those who hate Him and who were idolaters. To hate God is to fail to put God first. For example, Jesus said that you must hate your father and mother, your wife and children, and brother and your sister to follow Him. What he means is that He must be first. No one can take His place. Otherwise, it is idolatry. God is a jealous God. That is why Satan will use stubbornness or rebellion in a son or daughter to bring forth the generational iniquity.

Look for sinful patterns that are recognized in parents, grandparents, and great-grandparents. Watch for statements about your family such as, "Johnny likes to sow his wild oats just like his granddaddy," or, "Martha is a nervous wreck like her mother." Look for problems that afflict your family and have been a pattern for other generations. That can include a wide range of patterns. Some examples are, sexual sins of all kinds, alcoholism, abusive behavior, excessive fear, nervous breakdowns, suicide, compulsive behavior, addictions of all kinds, self-injury (cutting, etc.), love of money, deceptive tendencies, mental problems, strong rebellion, judgmentalism, idolatry, occultism, and false beliefs.

---

14 William B. Berman, Dale R. Doty, and Jean Huff Graham, *Shaking The Family Tree, Using Your Family's Past to Strengthen Your Family's Future* (Wheaton, IL: Victor Books, 1991), 29-31.

How to Break Generational Patterns

We live in the day of the new covenant, and with the power of Christ, these patterns do not need to continue.

In those days people will no longer say, 'The fathers have eaten sour grapes, and the children's teeth are set on edge.' Instead, everyone will die for his own sin; whoever eats sour grapes—his own teeth will be set on edge. "The time is coming," declares the LORD, "when I will make a new covenant with the house of Israel and with the house of Judah... (Jeremiah 31:29-31)

Step One   Identify one or more patterns of generational iniquities.

Step Two   Take time for godly sorrow to work. See it as God sees it. If you are involved directly, allow godly sorrow to work repentance.

Step Three   Repent of your sin if you are involved in one of these generational iniquities. A generational pattern is no excuse for known sin. Begin to walk in freedom from this sin.

Step Four   Reject the sins of the fathers. That does not mean that those who committed such sins will not stand before God on their behalf. What it does mean is that you identify with the transgressions and agree with God that it was sinful behavior and you will not welcome it any longer (Nehemiah 1:6; Daniel 9:8).

Step Five   Renounce that sin in the family line. If you can identify that transgression with a particular spirit, rebuke and command the spirit to leave the family line.

Step Six   Forgive your ancestors for opening the door to this family iniquity. Jesus gave us examples of forgiving when someone sins against us in their blindness of iniquity. Jesus said, "Father, forgive them, for they do not know what they are doing" (Luke 23:34).

Application

1. A generational iniquity speaks of a _tendency_ or _propensity_ for a particular weakness.

2. To how many generations will God visit iniquity upon those who hate Him?

   _3 - 4_

3. What sin can be seen in the generational line of Abraham?

   deceit

4. What sin can be found in the generational line of David?

   Sexual sin

5. Prayerfully examine your own life and family. Do you see any sinful patterns that are obvious?

   • Sexual Sins—incest, homosexuality, fornication, adultery, compulsive masturbation, frigidity, prostitution, pedophilia, pornography, exhibitionist, etc.

   • Addictions—drugs, alcohol, nicotine, gambling, eating disorder, compulsive behavior, wild living.

   • Occultism—witchcraft, astrology, clairvoyance, psychic control or healing, palm reading, superstition, tarot cards, Ouija board, voodoo, eastern meditation, and fortune telling.

   • False Religions—Atheism, false cults, secret societies, and idolatry (worship of other gods).

   • Sins of the Heart—rebellion, stubbornness, bitterness, judgmentalism, legalism, lust, pride, laziness, holding grudges, unloving, hatred, and prejudice.

   • Sins Against Others—abortion, murder, betrayal, covenant breaking (divorce), lying, manipulation or control, strife, thievery, cursing, gossiping, and fighting.

6. Apply the six steps to breaking generational patterns on the previous page to each sinful pattern that you have discovered.

Healing Your Past

There is little difference in counseling and personal ministry when the Word of God brings healing through the Holy Spirit. That is exactly what counseling should be. Most problems can be healed from our daily prayer time and growing in the Word of God. I can tell you that I have seen people change from simply hearing the truth and applying it to their lives. However, some deep-rooted areas of the past require more effort and time. For whatever reason, there has been a block or stronghold that has kept the Word of God and the Holy Spirit from touching that area. Some hurts are so deep that the help of others is required.

Step One—Identification

When a person identifies the wounds from the past and understands his inappropriate response to what has happened to him, he is well on his way to victory. The past wounds are no longer hidden. In His good time, God has revealed it for healing and restoration.

There are times when a person will lose memory of traumatic events in childhood. It is a coping mechanism. The pain of the past trauma is so severe, that person's mind has stuffed the memories away. After a period, those memories are lost. In a healthy environment, the child would be encouraged to talk about the trauma and, given time, process it all. When someone in authority carries out damaging behavior, a child may refuse or not be given the opportunity to process the deep hurt. In a poorly dysfunctional family, one of the rules is, "We don't talk about things like that."

Some possible evidence of hidden memories includes having unclear memories of childhood. That is not to say that people remember everything about their past because we don't, but if large portions of time are lost in childhood, that could be an indication of buried memories. The inability to experience certain feelings or having adverse reactions to a particular environment may disclose hidden memories. Often, when a person hears others tell of their own experiences and how they felt or suffered, it will trigger memories. Embrace these difficult moments to reveal the need for healing. Allow the Holy Spirit to reveal any hidden or suppressed memories.

You do not have to go looking for hidden memories. The Holy Spirit will bring forth those areas at the proper time. Being in an emotionally safe environment promotes emotional growth and health. Healthy people help others to choose to heal. Remember, Jesus was anointed by the Holy Spirit to heal the brokenhearted (Luke 4:18). The Holy Spirit will help you identify your need.

Step Two—Embracing

To embrace your past is a good indication that you are moving toward healing. To be healed you must allow yourself to feel those wounds. You cannot afford to run or hide from your past hurts anymore.

Write it or tell it. A good way to fully embrace your pain is to write it out or tell someone you trust. If you do not have an open and safe group or counselor, you can write a letter to Jesus. Tell Him every detail, how you felt, and what was going on in your mind at the time. Ask God to reveal to you what you should know or remember about the situation and include every aspect.

Release your emotions. Holding your emotions inside from the past hurts only keeps you in bondage. Allow yourself to express the emotion of fear, sadness, anger, resentment, etc. When you embrace the intensity of your hurt, you are allowing honesty to enter your pain. Tell God just how much you were hurt. By releasing your built-up emotions and allowing God to be your healer, you are also removing any barriers to forgiveness. You may want to confront the person who offended you by writing it in a letter, addressing the person by name, but never mailing it. In your forgiveness time, you can shred or burn the letter, allowing Jesus to fill the void in your life.

Step Three—Repenting

At first, the idea of needing to repent may seem completely wrong. This is an important step, however, because of bitterness, resentment, and anger. Even though you have been the one who has been injured, it is important to embrace your inappropriate response to what happened to you. Hurt internalized becomes depression; externalized it turns into hurtful anger. A root of bitterness becomes a bigger obstacle than the trauma itself. This applies in particular if the hurt is more from your perception, and you do not have an incident to describe. Though perception is real, it may be the bitterness that is causing the destruction.

Addressing Bitterness

1. Ask God to forgive you for the sin of bitterness. Say, "Heavenly Father, I have sinned by holding onto bitterness in my life. I ask You to forgive me for a sin of bitterness against (place the person's name in the blank.)"

2. Ask God to restore the emotional ground that you have lost since the bitterness came into your life. Ask Him to heal any other part of your life that has been defiled by bitterness. Say, "Father, I ask You to restore to me the emotional growth and health that I have lost because of my bitterness. Heal every part of my life that has been defiled by this bitterness."

3. Ask God to remove the transgression from that person's account. Say, "Father, I ask You not to hold this sin against (person's name). I release (person's name) from this debt."

Step Four—Forgiving

Forgiveness can be offered when you realize that you have been forgiven. The Bible instructs us to forgive as the Lord Jesus forgave you (Colossians 3:13). What does it mean to forgive? To forgive does not mean that you will forget. You will remember the event, but you will be freed from the pain. Forgiveness means that you choose not to bring it up again. The memory is healed so that it becomes redemptive. Your feelings will follow your decision to forgive. The struggle with that person will be gone, and you will be left with a sense of wholeness in that area.

Forgiveness Test

1. Is there resentment? If you have a strong resentment toward that person, then you know that you have not received healing. You may even experience compassion for the person after you forgive, realizing that he or she is in bondage with their sin.

2. Are you blaming? If you are still blaming others for your present condition, then you probably have not forgiven. Hearing yourself use "if only" statements, indicate you have not entered into the healing process.

3. Is there an association? If you are reacting to a person because they remind you of someone else, then you are still dealing with a deep wound. Wounded people project their pain on others. A wounded heart forms judgments.

Step Five—Growing

Learn to draw from adverse circumstances. You do not have to fear life itself because Christ your healer is living in you. Continue to grow in God's love for you and His desire for you to be whole.

What are you learning about yourself? What you know about yourself is important for your personal growth. Be prepared to discuss this with the person helping to disciple you in Christ.

Application

1. In your own words, tell why it is important to identify past hurts in order to be healed.

_____

_____

_____

2. What are some of the possible evidences of hidden memories?

_____

_____

_____

3. There are two aspects of embracing your hurt. What are they?

_____

_____

_____

4. Write out the three steps to addressing bitterness. After writing these out, take time to apply this to anyone that you may have resentment toward.

    1) _____

    2) _____

    3) _____

5. What are the three aspects of the forgiveness test?

    1) _____

    2) _____

    3) _____

6. Go to this week's memory verse and spend some time meditating on these verses.

Overcoming in Christ

I remember when I was a boy and friends of my father and mother came to visit our church occasionally. This couple also served in the ministry pastoring. Dad would always ask the wife to sing. She was short in stature, but even more so because of polio. She would pull herself up on crutches, move slowly to the front of the church, and sit down on the altar with her crutches at her side. Then, without music or accompaniment, she would begin to sing, "He was wounded for our transgressions, He was bruised for our iniquity, surely He bore our sorrows, and by His stripes, we are healed." Never did I hear her sing except she sang that same song, and never did she sing except the glory of God was on her face. Though she never received her physical healing, I knew she knew the Healer.

In the same way, we must come to the altar and know the healer. We must come to Jesus for our healing while we are still in our affliction and know that He bore our sorrows.

Jesus Relates

The book of Hebrews tells us that Jesus was our substitute in every way. We can come boldly before His throne of grace in the time of need (Hebrews 4:15, 16). He is acquainted with our grief. He knows our weaknesses. He understands what it means to hurt. Jesus was God in the flesh. By becoming human, He identified with your humanity. When you find someone who has gone through the same things that you have, there is an affinity, a feeling of closeness, and identification with the struggle. That is the way it is with Jesus with us. You can come to Him knowing that He knows your pain. Jesus took upon Himself the entire range of our wounds.

He Relates to the Sorrowful Soul

When Jesus went to the Garden of Gethsemane, He experienced great sorrow. He was in great agony of spirit. He knows what it is like to cry. He knows what it is like to weep with sobs. He has been through deep sorrow. When you come to Jesus with sorrow, He knows your pain. The Bible tells us,

During the days of Jesus' life on earth, he offered up prayers and petitions with loud cries and tears to the one who could save him from death, and he was heard because of his reverent submission. Although he was a son, he learned obedience from what he suffered. (Hebrews 5:7, 8)

It cost Jesus a lot to be our substitute. As our healer, Jesus walked through much suffering. Go with Jesus to the garden. Hear Him cry out to the Father. He said that His soul was overwhelmed with sorrow to the point of death (Matt 26:38). What pain He must have suffered to be considered close to dying. His emotional pain was as great as anyones. In one of the prophetic Messianic Psalms, it speaks of our Lord. Can you see Jesus' distress in reading this?

> *I sink in the miry depths, where there is no foothold. I have come into the deep waters; the floods engulf me. I am worn out calling for help; my throat is parched. My eyes fail, looking for my God. . . . Scorn has broken my heart and has left me helpless; I looked for sympathy, but there was none, for comforters, but I found none. (Psalm 69:2, 3, 20)*

When Jesus asked His disciples to stay awake and pray with Him, they did not. When they came for Jesus, all forsook Him. He knows the loneliness of rejection and betrayal from those who are the closest.

He Relates to Humiliation and Abuse

Go with Jesus to His trial. Watch what authorities and bystanders do to Him. Few things hurt as deeply as a false judgment of motives. I have seen the deep wounds that come to people because of false accusations. Jesus knows what it means to be wrongfully accused. At His trial those in authority wrongfully and harshly accused him. He was beaten to near death. He was mocked and ridiculed as they acted out their scorn. Jesus has been called every name that you have been called. Jesus can relate.

They tormented and humiliated Jesus by hitting Him on the head and across the face. Imagine the dishonor from being slapped across the face. They spat in His face and mocked Him. Jesus bore it all, and He did it for you and in your place.

He Relates to Isolation and Death

On the cross, Jesus suffered the rejection of all. He knows how you feel when you have been jilted by someone close to you, ridiculed by a group, and shunned by all. The prophet Isaiah tells us,

> *He had no beauty or majesty to attract us to him, nothing in his appearance that we should desire him. He was despised and rejected by men, a man of sorrows, and familiar with suffering. Like one from whom men hide their faces he was despised, and we esteemed him not. (Isaiah 53:2, 3)*

When Jesus became sin for you, He was cut off from God. He cried out, but God did not answer Him. He knows what it is like to suffer alone and to feel like prayers are not heard. We know this is true of Scripture. The Palmist David wrote, "My God, my God, why have you forsaken me? Why are you so far from saving me, so far from the words of my groaning? O my God, I cry out by day, but you do not answer. . . "(Psalm 22:1, 2).

At your lowest moments of rejection and your darkest hour, Jesus has been there. He even relates to the feelings of being cut off from God. You need not be afraid to come to Jesus with your hurts. He is your healer and understands and is touched by your infirmities.

Jesus Heals Broken Hearts

There is no reason for you to hesitate to come to Jesus with a broken heart. Not only does He relate to your pain and suffering, but He also desires to heal the brokenhearted and free those who are down-trodden. The Gospel of Luke quotes Isaiah,

> *"The Spirit of the Lord is upon me; he has anointed me to preach Good News to the poor; he has sent me to heal the brokenhearted and to announce that captives shall be released and the blind shall see, that the downtrodden shall be freed from their oppressors, and that God is ready to give blessings to all who come to him."* (Luke 4:18)

If you are in need of healing, today is your day. Allow your heart to be open to Jesus. Some healing will come quickly, and some will be over a period of time. However, Christ remains your healer. Know you are loved, and He is present to heal.

Application

1. We know that Jesus knew great sorrow. Give one verse that lets you know that He relates to your sorrow. Write it out.

   Ps. 22 1-2

2. Many people have suffered from false accusations. If you have ever suffered false accusation, physical abuse, or emotional abuse, what was it like? Describe your emotion related to that event.

   When I was in 3rd grade my teacher made fun of me put me down in front of the class

3. If a loved one has rejected you, describe that emotion.

   you don't feel good about yourself, but really it ok God is using that situation for a purpose

4. Take each wound to Jesus. Knowing that He relates to your suffering, allow Him to touch your life. See Jesus in your situation ministering healing to your loss. Take time to allow the Holy Spirit to work healing in your life.

Our Father's Love

Over the years of pastoral ministry, I have seen so many who have been adversely affected by the absence of a father's love, or at least a perception of the lack thereof. There is something powerful about the relationship of the father to children. It is vital for each Christian to have a fresh revelation of the heavenly Father's love.

Some who are reading this material may not even know their father. Some grew up in a broken home where they experienced feelings of abandonment. Others may have experienced an unexpressive father who never told them they were loved, or even worse, told they could never be loved. Consequently, it is difficult for some who have had such experiences to believe that God loves them. In truth, because of the sinful nature, all those who come to Christ must have a revelation of the Father's love to fully grow into what God has purposed, regardless of their upbringing.

The story of the father's love toward the prodigal son is such an expression of what God's love is toward you. Read the following passage slowly.

> There was a man who had two sons. The younger one said to his father, "Father, give me my share of the estate." So he divided his property between them. Not long after that, the younger son got together all he had, set off for a distant country, and there squandered his wealth in wild living. After he had spent everything, there was a severe famine in that whole country, and he began to be in need. So he went and hired himself out to a citizen of that country, who sent him to his fields to feed pigs. He longed to fill his stomach with the pods that the pigs were eating, but no one gave him anything. When he came to his senses, he said, "How many of my father's hired men have food to spare, and here I am starving to death! I will set out and go back to my father and say to him: Father, I have sinned against heaven and against you. I am no longer worthy to be called your son; make me like one of your hired men." So he got up and went to his father. But while he was still a long way off, his father saw him and was filled with compassion for him; he ran to his son, threw his arms around him and kissed him. The son said to him, "Father, I have sinned against heaven and against you. I am no longer worthy to be called your son." But the father said to his servants, "Quick! Bring the best robe and put it on him. Put a ring on his finger and sandals on his feet. Bring the fattened calf and kill it. Let's have a feast and celebrate. For this son of mine was dead and is alive again; he was lost and is found." So they began to celebrate. (Luke 15:11-24)

The Son's Response

The wayward son's first response was that he changed his mind. That was the first sign of repentance. He came to his senses. Sin can block the reasoning. That is the way you were when you came to Christ. Without the heavenly Father, your emotional life is in a fog. When this son saw the error of his ways, he must have asked himself a hundred times, "What was I thinking?"

When he changed his mind, he decided that he would go home to his father. His thinking had changed, and now his decisions were different. He prepared in advance what he would say. He knew he must acknowledge that he had sinned against heaven and his father. Repentance was working in him.

The son changed his attitude. He was humbled. As this son's attention turned from his own destructive decisions, he began to remember how his father took care of even the servants. He saw a mental picture of how it could be for himself. The son returned with a change in his thinking and his attitude.

The Father's Response

The father saw the son returning. The father saw him at a great distance because he was watching for him. The father's heart never turned from his son. Even though the son had left the love of the father, the father never stopped loving his son. No matter what you have done, God's heart has never turned from you. His love is unconditional.

When the father saw his son returning, he was moved emotionally. The father was filled with compassion for his son and ran toward him. He threw his arms around his son and embraced him. The father held his son close and began to kiss him. At this point, nothing was different about the son except his thinking and decisions. Repentance was working in him. He was still in dirty clothes, without shoes, and wondering about his worth or place. The father's love began to transform the son. It melted away the rebellion and hardness. All was changed in the loving arms of the father. It is not until we are embraced with the love of our merciful Father that we go through a change or conversion. While the son tried to tell the father that he was not worthy to be his son and begged to be a servant, the father ignored those words and continued to embrace and kiss him. The father pronounced value and blessing on his son and restoration began to take place.

Even while the son objected, the father called for the family robe to be placed on his son, changing his status from an outsider to a family member. The father restored the son to his rightful place. He placed the best clean robe on this dirty son. He did not require him to have a shower first. This robe represents God's righteousness and His covering of our sin. It means that when he places his robe on us, the dirt and the past is gone. He is not afraid to place his righteousness on us because he knows the transforming power of God's love.

The father also restored the son's full authority. Though the son was willing to be a servant, the father would have it no other way than to have his son in his rightful place. He placed the family ring on his finger. The same hand that had handled the prostitutes was now given the highest honor of authority. The hand that had stiff-armed all his dad's values was now receiving this very expensive and powerful ring. It was a signet ring showing that he was a son of this very wealthy father. Though he had spent much of the father's wealth on sinful living, the father included him back into the inheritance. He could now go to the marketplace and buy and trade with his father's authority as if he had never left. What forgiveness the father bestowed upon his son.

When the father saw his son without shoes, he restored his son to the family position by placing sandals on his son's feet. A slave went without shoes. His father was determined he was not a slave but a son. He gave him right standing with the family. He restored him fully.

The father celebrated. Rather than rub his son's sin in his face, he chose to forgive and place the past behind him. The power of the father's love for his son made him more valuable and important than what the son had done. The father threw a party and celebrated his son's return.

Place yourself in the circumstances of this prodigal son. In your mind see the heavenly Father waiting and watching for your return. Feel the Father's embrace and kisses, even while you try to object. Hear Him call for the best robe, the family ring, and sandals for your bare feet. Let the Father melt your stubbornness and hardness away. Where sin and life's troubles have left you defeated and lonely, allow the Father's kisses to restore you to the place of righteousness that He has provided for you.

It does not matter what you have done or what has happened to you, the healing power of the Father's love is the answer to your life. The heavenly Father's love can displace any wound from your past.

Application

1. Describe your relationship with your earthly father.

It was my dad never told us he loved us but would always give us things And would tell us to always work hard

2. What was the first evidence of repentance for the prodigal son?

for him coming home

3. The son not only had a change in his thinking but also in his _heart_.

4. Go through the story of the father's love for the prodigal son. Identify each aspect of the father's response.

   1) The father ___saw___ the son returning.

   2) The father saw the son returning because he had been ___looking___ for him.

   3) When he saw his son, he was moved with ___Compassion___.

   4) While the son was insisting that he was not worthy, what was the father doing?

   loving on him

   5) What did the father first place on his son? ___ring___

   6) What did the robe represent?

   from outsider ⬤ to a family member

   7) How did the father restore the son's authority?

   placing a ring on his finger

   8) Why was it so special that the father placed sandals on his son's feet?

   he was no longer a slave

5. Take time to meditate upon this powerful Bible story and allow the Holy Spirit to reveal the Father's love to you. Ask Him to touch your heart and life.

Chosen by The Father

Everyone desires to be chosen. No one wants to be left out. Belonging is very important to each one of us. That is why it is important to know just how much the heavenly Father loves you. Since He loves you, He has chosen to include you with every spiritual blessing.

> *Praise be to the God and Father of our Lord Jesus Christ, who has blessed us in the heavenly realms with every spiritual blessing in Christ. For he chose us in him before the creation of the world to be holy and blameless in his sight. In love he predestined us to be adopted as his sons through Jesus Christ, in accordance with his pleasure and will—to the praise of his glorious grace, which he has freely given us in the One he loves. (Ephesians 1:3-6)*

People often say, "The truth shall set you free." Well, that is partially correct. What Jesus said was, "You shall know the truth, and the truth shall set you free" (John 8:32). The operative word is *know*. If you know who you are in Christ, and what He has done for you, it will transform your life. This is an experiential knowledge by the Holy Spirit, not just head knowledge.

Paul knew how important it was for Christians to have this revelation to be secure and stand strong in the face of challenges. He wrote to the Christians at Ephesus while he was in prison in Rome with this understanding. His purpose in writing was to keep the Church from falling into the secular cultural philosophies that surrounded them. The temple of the goddess Diana was located in Ephesus. There was a lot of darkness in the form of spirituality in their culture. The Christians were subject to being deceived if they did not know these "in-Him realities." That is why he spoke so clearly of being chosen by the Father.

Chosen in Christ

You are not chosen based on your merits or your worthiness, but rather on Christ's merits. The term "in Christ" as used in the Scriptures is more than just a technical term. That is not just a figure of speech. It is a present reality. This speaks of the relationship that exists between you and Christ. It means that God has identified you with His Son. You are made holy and treated the same as Jesus is treated from the Father's perspective. Father God chose us in Christ before the world was formed.

Chosen Before the World Was Formed

One of God's mysteries is that even before the world was founded and before Adam and Eve were created, God chose His people in Christ to be holy and blameless in his sight (Ephesians 1:5). *The*

Pulpit Commentary states, "The work of redemption was planned and its details arranged from all eternity."[15] The Scriptures teach us that Christ was also chosen as the sacrifice to die for our sins before the creation of the world (1 Peter 1:18, 19). Nothing speaks more of us being chosen than this sacred truth that you were chosen in Him before the world was framed.

Chosen to Be Holy and Without Blame

God did not choose you because you were good enough to be selected. His purpose in choosing you was to bring you to holiness and for Christ's image to be formed in you. Christ declares you holy when you believe, but then you grow in your walk or experience of holiness throughout your lifetime. Paul explained by saying, "And we all, who with unveiled faces contemplate the Lord's glory, are being transformed into his image with ever-increasing glory, which comes from the Lord, who is the Spirit" (2 Corinthians 3:18). Your spiritual growth into His image is ever-increasing.

Paul's desire for the Thessalonians was that the God of peace would sanctify them through and through, and keep them blameless (1 Thessalonians 5:23). To be without blame denotes that you are not marked or stained by the imperfections of sin. Christ has removed that from you. This can only be in Christ's forgiveness and by His grace, not of our works of righteousness. When the Father looks at you, He not only sees your sins forgiven, but the righteous record of Jesus' life is in the place of your old record. Where your sins once were marked against you, now Jesus' record of holiness is applied to you. The Father has declared you holy in the scrutiny of His sight. Therefore, the reality of the position of holiness is "in Christ." It is from that positional holiness that you are called to continue to walk by the same grace into a mature Christian.

Chosen to Be Adopted

The fact that we are adopted into God's family as children points to the love relationship and closeness that we have with the Father. It is a family affair. The Scriptures use familial expressions when referring to our relationships. It is the family of God. The terms, God the Father, Jesus the Son, the Church as the bride, and the fact we are brothers and sisters to each other, all point to the family relationship. Our adoption is more than a legal reality; it is a relational one as God's children. The Gospel of John declares, "Yet to all who received him, to those who believed in his name, he gave the right to become children of God" (John 1:12).

Paul says that God predestined us to be adopted as his sons through Jesus Christ. To be predestined means to be "marked out" or "specified." Part of the mystery of God is that He moves to bring forth His will without violating ours. That can only be said of God. God's sovereignty does not take away your free will; rather, He moves upon your will. No one is dragged kicking and screaming to God; they

---

15 H. D. Spense and Joseph S. Exell, *The Pulpit Commentary* (Grand Rapids, MI: Wm. B. Eerdmans Publishing Company, 1975), Ephesians p. 2.

come running to Him out of their desire. No one is saved against their will, yet God draws people to Himself. Jesus said, "No one can come to me unless the Father who sent me draws them" (John 6:44). From our perspective it is "our choice," and it is. From God's perspective it is "His choice," and it is. Our faith that comes from God is a response from our will which He has moved upon. We cannot speculate beyond that. We can only accept the Word of God as our authority, knowing that His judgments are unsearchable, and His ways beyond finding out (Romans 11:33).

Chosen According to His Pleasure

The motive to choose you is of God Himself. Though it pleases us to be chosen, that is not the reason we are called. You have been marked for adoption because it pleased God. It may be hard for you to believe it is for God's pleasure that He has chosen you, yet that is the truth. It is according to His divine plan and for His praise. Your worthiness is of His choosing. If you look only at your shortcomings and the difficulties of your life, you will soon come up short and feel the rejection of the highest order. However, once you understand the Father's love and His choice of your life, you will begin to see your value from God's perspective. It gives praise and glory to God when we delight in His grace and accept His calling on our lives. This is holy ground.

The Bible tells us God chooses, calls, justifies, and glorifies His people according to His purpose. Paul explains it further by saying,

> And we know that in all things God works for the good of those who love him, who have been called according to his purpose. For those God foreknew he also predestined to be conformed to the image of his Son, that he might be the firstborn among many brothers and sisters. And those he predestined, he also called; those he called, he also justified; those he justified, he also glorified. (Romans 8:28-30)

Application

1. Read Ephesians 1:3-6. Read it several times until you can give back the general meaning of what is being said. Write your thoughts from that passage.

   That we are adopted by Jesus Christ he loved us way be time & when we chose him, then he is our father we go to for everything

2. Explain what "in Christ" means.

   He is everything to me I love him so much

3. Read 1 Peter 1:18, 19. What thought stands out the most to you?

   God chose us

4. What are some of the terms used in the Bible to describe the family of God?

5. Give some of the feelings or emotions that come to mind when you meditate upon the idea that it pleased God to choose you.

   There are no words but gratitude & honor he love us

6. Go to the appendix for the memory verses for this week and work on memorizing them.

Redeemed by The Son

By now you are growing in the knowledge of what Christ has done for you.

The purpose of today's lesson is to build upon that knowledge concerning the redemptive work of Christ. This lesson should birth a deep appreciation for your salvation.

Paul wrote to the Ephesians with a desire for them to know that the Father chose them and that God had lavished on them His redemptive grace through His Son, Jesus. Paul wrote to the Christians in Ephesus saying, "In him we have redemption through his blood, the forgiveness of sins, in accordance with the riches of God's grace that he lavished on us with all wisdom and understanding" (Ephesians 1:7, 8).

The word redemption means to buy or purchase. We must ask, what motivated God to pay such a high cost for our redemption? What were the means of this purchase? Who did He pay? And, what was involved in our redemption?

The Motive for Redemption

The Bible tells us to consider the kindness and sternness of God. His sternness toward those who fell, but His kindness to those who believe (Romans 11:22). His character reveals both His love and justice. Both of these point to the motive for your redemption. It was love, in that "God so loved the world that He gave His only Son, that whoever believes in Him should not perish but have everlasting life" (John 3:16). Through Adam's sin, we all were separated from God. Christ died for us when we were enemies of God. Paul wrote, "But God demonstrates His own love for us in this: While we were still sinners, Christ died for us" (Romans 5:8).

Justice was also the cause of our redemption in that a penalty had to be paid for the sin. God in His holiness would not change His character and join with darkness. After the fall, Adam and Eve were driven from the Garden. The elements of redemption were put into place through His love and justice. The sins committed in the Old Testament were forgiven looking toward the coming Messiah, but the penalty had not been paid until Christ. Paul says this is the reason that Jesus was sent as a sacrifice of atonement.

> *God presented him as a sacrifice of atonement, through faith in his blood. He did this to demonstrate his justice, because in his forbearance he had left the sins committed beforehand unpunished—he did it to demonstrate his justice at the present time, so as to be just and the one who justifies those who have faith in Jesus. (Romans 3:25, 26)*

It was love and justice that motivated God to send His Son for our redemption. He did not have to provide salvation. God could have left all of humanity in their sinful state eternally doomed and He would have been just to have done so. The Bible says, "God did not spare angels when they sinned, but sent them to hell, putting them into gloomy dungeons to be held for judgment" (2 Peter 2:4). In the same manner, God was under no requirement or compulsion to redeem His bride other than from His love and for His glory. The price he paid was out of love and justice through the sacrifice of Jesus on the cross.

The Means of Redemption

For our redemption to come to pass several elements had to be in place. Once God determined to redeem humanity, it required a perfect sacrifice as holy as He. God alone is holy, so He provided for Himself a perfect lamb, His own son. God created Adam and Eve in His image and His perfect righteousness without sin. When man fell into sin in the Garden of Eden, Jesus was the only pure qualified sacrifice to take on the burden of sin. He chose to die under the penalty of the Law and experience separation from Father God, as was the state of fallen man.

Christ suffered obedience His entire life: From the time of Adam, man has fallen and lived a life of sin. Jesus who was sinless became a man and lived out His life where Adam and Eve had failed. Jesus lived His life here on earth in total obedience without sin. It is hard not to get your own way but to trust. Jesus experienced the suffering of obedience (Hebrews 5:8). Jesus lived a life of obedience throughout His entire time on earth and earned righteousness for us. When we put our faith in Christ, we are credited with His righteous merits and perfect life. Jesus not only died for our sins; He lived out our righteousness so we might share in His righteous life as if we lived it in obedience ourselves. We do not have, nor trust in, our own righteousness which is based on the Law, but the righteousness that is through faith in Christ (Philippians 3:9).

Christ suffered the pain of the cross: His obedience led Him to the agony of the soul in the Garden of Gethsemane and then to the cross. Death by crucifixion under the Romans was one of the most horrible forms of execution imaginable. He suffered in our place the pain of a sinner's death.

Christ suffered the burden of sin: More agonizing than the physical pain of the cross was the bearing of sin for mankind. He had to take on the psychological, emotional, and mental pain of the anguish of sin. We as sinners have known the weightiness of our sin, but none can imagine the sinless Christ being made sin for the whole world. He who knew no sin was made to be sin for us (2 Corinthians 5:21). We hate the effects of sin and even hate sin itself, but Christ who was the opposite of sin was made to become our sin. The prophet Isaiah writes, "The LORD has laid on Him the iniquity of us all" (Isaiah 53:6). God the Father, put our sins on Christ in the same way that Adam's sin was imputed to us. Our sins were credited to Jesus, and His righteousness came to us. God did not consider Jesus to have committed the sins, but the liability was counted as belonging to Christ.

Christ suffered abandonment: If the agony of the cross was horrific, imagine the isolation and abandonment that Jesus would have felt in dying alone. It was outside the city among criminals where Jesus was crucified. His disciples had forsaken Him in the hour of darkness. More than any human rejection was the moment the Father turned from His Son because of our sin. Jesus trusted the Father, but the agony of separation and abandonment was not lessened. His cry was, "My God, My God, why have You forsaken me?" The eternal communion of God the Father, and the second member of the Godhead was severed for the first and only time in all eternity. For that period Jesus bore our sins alone.

Christ suffered God's anger: As a just and holy God, there had to be a sacrifice that was qualified to meet His requirement. Up until the cross, the punishment or "atonement" for sin had been stored up through God's longsuffering, and His righteous anger had been held back. At the cross, the fury of God's wrath against sin was discharged on His own Son. Jesus suffered the penalty for our sins. He took our place on the cross. The Father inflicted our penalty on Him. For our sakes, it pleased the Father to bruise His Son in our place (Isaiah 53:10). Our ransom was paid to free us from the bondage of sin. Though we were in bondage to sin and Satan, the penalty was not paid to Satan, but rather to God Himself. The ransom was the price required to meet the holy requirement of a holy God for our sin.

Redemption through Christ is the central theme of the Bible. The Bible tells us the reason Christ came to this earth was to destroy the works of the devil (1 John 3:8). To accomplish this feat, God came in the flesh and became human to deliver us from Satan's hold and pay the price of atonement for our sins to meet His holy requirement. The writer of Hebrews explains Christ's work, "For this reason he had to be made like them, fully human in every way, in order that he might become a merciful and faithful high priest in service to God, and that he might make atonement for the sins of the people" (Hebrews 2:17).

Application

1. God's character reveals both _____ and _____.

2. What verse tells us that God demonstrated His love for us while we were still sinners?

   _____

3. What verse tells us that God demonstrated His justice?

   _____

4. There were five means of Christ's suffering in our redemption. Identify each one and give a summary in your own words.

   1) Christ suffered
      Christ suffered obedience, his
      entire life

   2) Christ suffered
      Christ suffered the pain on the
      cross

   3) Christ suffered
      Christ suffered the burden of
      sin

   4) Christ suffered
      he suffered abandonment

   5) Christ suffered
      Christ suffered God's anger

Sealed by The Holy Spirit

We are not only chosen by the Father and redeemed by the Son, but the Holy Spirit seals us until the day of redemption. In Paul's letter to the Ephesians, he explains the work of the Holy Spirit who guarantees our inheritance.

> *And you also were included in Christ when you heard the word of truth, the Gospel of your salvation. Having believed, you were marked in Him with a seal, the promised Holy Spirit, who is a deposit guaranteeing our inheritance until the redemption of those who are God's possession—to the praise of his glory.* (Ephesians 1:13, 14)

Having heard the Gospel, you were marked in Christ with a seal. This seal is none other than the Holy Spirit who came to live in you when you received your salvation. What does it mean to be sealed? Paul uses this term three times in His Epistles to reveal the work of the Spirit to guarantee our salvation.[16]

Seal of Authentication

To authenticate something is to certify it as valid. We see an example of such in the Scriptures when John the Baptist was speaking of those who accept Christ; they authenticate that He is true. He writes, "The man who has accepted it has certified that God is truthful" (John 3:33). John declares that a believer certifies that God is not a liar because he experiences God's life.

In the same sense, the Holy Spirit certifies that we are Christians. In other words, the mark of a Christian is the presence of the Holy Spirit. The seal of the Holy Spirit is God's way of certifying the fact that one is a true Christian. Paul says, "The Spirit himself testifies with our spirit that we are God's children" (Romans 8:16).

A person may claim to be a Christian, go through the words and give intellectual assent to the truth of the Gospel, and not necessarily be a Christian. There have been many who have testified of being raised in a Christian home or serving in a church environment, and later discover they did not have a witness of God's presence in their lives. After receiving the assurance of the Spirit, they were able to recognize they had been without the seal of the Spirit. The proof of being a child of God is the presence of the Holy Spirit in the life of a believer.

---

16 2 Corinthians 1:22; 5:5; Ephesians 1:13, 14

Seal of Authorization

The Scriptures declare as Christians we belong to God and that Jesus is the author of our salvation (Hebrews 2:10). The Holy Spirit is the seal of that authority and ownership. For God has "set his seal of ownership on us, and put his Spirit in our hearts as a deposit, guaranteeing what is to come" (2 Corinthians 1:22).

To authorize something is to place a stamp of ownership on it as with a seal. The Holy Spirit is a seal of deposit, guaranteeing the full redemption of those who are His possession. Peter tells us we belong to God. He declares, "But you are a chosen people, a royal priesthood, a holy nation, a people belonging to God, that you may declare the praises of him who called you out of darkness into his wonderful light" (1 Peter 2:9).

Only those who belong to God can receive the Holy Spirit. God gives His Spirit to His possession (Ephesians 1:14). The Holy Spirit reveals God's ownership and guarantees what is to come. Now the one who has fashioned us for this very purpose is God, who has given us the Spirit as a deposit, guaranteeing what is to come.

Seal of Assurance

You can have assurance you are a Christian because you have received an earnest deposit of the Spirit. This seal is our assurance that our full inheritance as children of God will be delivered. When a contract is made to purchase a large item, earnest money or a deposit is often required. A deposit seals the contract until delivery is made of the item. The Holy Spirit is that guarantee of our inheritance until the full redemption of those who are God's possession. The deposit that God has given as His assurance is Himself. Think about how marvelous that is for such a valuable deposit to be given as your assurance. When God made the promise to Abraham, He swore to Himself because there was no one greater. God's promise is not only to you but to Himself on your behalf. The writer of Hebrews explains, "When God made His promise to Abraham, since He had no one greater to swear by, He swore by Himself" (Hebrews 6:13).

What an excellent thought—that the Holy Spirit is our absolute guarantee. He is the pledge from Father God. When the Bible speaks of redemption, it includes the completed work of Christ on your behalf, which you received at the time of regeneration, and it extends unto the resurrection of the body at the time of Christ's return. Paul said, ". . . we ourselves, who have the firstfruits of the Spirit, groan inwardly as we wait eagerly for our adoption as sons, the redemption of our bodies" (Romans 8:23).

The fact that we have received the seal of the Holy Spirit is our promise for the present reality and our future inheritance. God grants to us His Spirit as a pledge that we are His and He will keep us. This guarantee carries over beyond this life even to the life to come. When our present bodies wear out, we can be confident that God has prepared for us a new body in the resurrection. We have a promise of what is to come. Paul tells us, "Now it is God who has made us for this very purpose and has given us the Spirit as a deposit, guaranteeing what is to come" (2 Corinthians 5:5).

Our hope goes beyond this life. The same Holy Spirit that raised you from spiritual death to eternal life is the same Spirit that will raise your mortal body in the resurrection. Paul writes, "And if the Spirit of Him who raised Jesus from the dead is living in you, He who raised Christ from the dead will also give life to your mortal bodies because of His Spirit who lives in you" (Romans 8:11). As wonderful as the Christian experience is, Paul tells the Corinthian Church that if we only have hope in this life we are to be pitied (1 Corinthians 15:19). Our promise in Christ includes the resurrection of our bodies. Paul continues to explain the resurrection of the dead,

> For as in Adam all die, so in Christ all will be made alive. But each in turn: Christ, the first-fruits; then, when He comes, those who belong to Him. Then the end will come, when He hands over the kingdom to God the Father after he has destroyed all dominion, authority and power. For He must reign until He has put all His enemies under His feet. The last enemy to be destroyed is death. (1 Corinthians 15:22-26)

The deposit of the Spirit authenticates our new birth, reveals His authority of ownership of our lives, and seals us until the day of redemption. The seal of deposit is the certainty of His love. We have the promise that this, "Hope does not disappoint us, because God has poured out His love into our hearts by the Holy Spirit, whom He has given us" (Romans 5:5).

The assurance we have with the Holy Spirit reminds me of the great hymn written by Fanny J. Crosby.

> Blessed assurance, Jesus is mine!
> O what a foretaste of glory divine!
> Heir of salvation, purchase of God,
> Born of His Spirit, washed in His blood.

Love it

Application

1. Having heard the Gospel, you were marked in Christ with a ___Seal___.

2. To authenticate something is to ___declaras___ it as valid.

3. How can a person know he is a Christian?

   When you ask Jesus into your heart & want to follow after him & do what the bible says

4. What does the seal of authorization mean? (2 Corinthians 1:22)

   that means he owns us we are not our anymore he put his spirit & heart into us like a deposit

5. What is an earnest deposit?

   large amount of money or deposit

6. We not only have the assurance of belonging to God, but we know that we have the firstfruits of the Spirit, and we are waiting for something to come. What are we waiting for?

   his Coming

7. Read 2 Corinthians 5:1-5. Rewrite in your own words the central thought from that passage.

   He "God" has made a deposit in us which means everything that God has written in our books-rev. Should come to pass if we run after God

Overcoming with the Word

No doubt, by now you are very much aware of how important God's Word is to your daily victories. You may have already been able to see yourself growing as a result of applying the Word of God to your life. One common denominator in each lesson so far has been the vital part that God's Word plays in our means of overcoming. Whether it is overcoming the world, flesh, sin, or the devil, the Word of God, along with God's Spirit, is the key to victory. The significance of the Bible in the life of a Christian cannot be overemphasized.

The Covenants

One of the first things that a person notices about his Bible is that there are two parts—the Old Testament and the New Testament. The first part is about God working through events and personalities to bring forth the purpose of Christ through His people who are called the children of God. The second part of the Bible deals with the events surrounding the birth, life of Jesus, and the subsequent beginnings of the Church as the body of Christ and Christ victorious reign.

A another word for a testament is a covenant. Kenneth Gentry, in his book *He Shall Have Dominion*, defines a covenant:

> A covenant may be defined as a legal bond, which establishes a favorable relation between parties based on certain specific terms, and which promises blessings for faithful adherence to those terms, while threatening curses for man's unfaithful departure from them.[17]

In revealing God's promise to use He has done so through His covenants. We have an "Old Covenant" and a "New Covenant" in the Bible. The first covenant became explicit under Moses with the commandments of God. The Mosaic covenant made at Mount Sinai with all its laws was given to restrain sin and be a custodian to point men to Christ (Galatians 3:19, 24). The "new" covenant was ratified through the blood of Jesus Christ. God is a covenant keeping God; therefore, He deals with His people through His covenant. The Bible is about His covenant. This is not a covenant made between two equals; rather it is made by God for Himself and for His people. The Bible is a record of that covenant relationship. The covenant finds its fulfillment and full expression in Jesus Christ. The Old Covenant faded and became obsolete when it was completed in Christ (Hebrews 8:13). The Old was not annulled or abolished but was fulfilled in Christ (Matthew 5:17). The New Covenant is the embodiment of the Old Covenant. The old *speaks* of Christ and the new *reveals* Christ (John 5:39).

---

17 Kenneth L. Gentry Jr., *He Shall Have Dominion* (Tyler, TX: Institute for Christian Economics, 1992), 106.

The Promise

God made numerous covenants with different individuals throughout the Old Testament, but there was only one promise. Only the covenant made with Moses at Mount Sinai is called the "Old Covenant." Paul refers to the "covenants of the promise" (Ephesians 2:12). Beginning with Adam in the creation of the world, the elements of a covenant were present. God established a legal bond with the promise of life for obedience and death for disobedience. In the story of the fall of man, we see the promise of the covenant expressed. The promise made was that the seed of a woman would crush the head of the serpent (Genesis 3:15). This signifies Jesus' death on the cross and His victory over the devil. Abraham also received the promise that his "seed" would bless all the families of the earth (Genesis 12:3). Paul tells us in Galatians 3:16, that the "seed" is Jesus Christ. The promise pointed to Christ, but the Old Covenant was made precise at Mount Sinai and with the commands given to Moses. The commands of God, summarized in the Ten Commandments, expressed His expectation of the covenant agreement. God demanded holy obedience in His covenant.

The first four commands of the Ten Commandments clarified specific obligations to God and the last six relate to man's responsibility to man. That is why Jesus summarized the Ten Commandments in two parts, "Love the Lord your God with all your heart and your neighbor as yourself" (Matthew 22:37-39). The Law of Moses is the clear requirement of the Holy God for a holy people.

This promise continued through King David. As one writer puts it,

> After King David, the covenant was linked with him and his descendants in Judah. It was the same covenant that had been binding upon Israel from the beginning, but now it was identified with the promise of an unbroken succession through the Davidic line. When the Davidic line ended with the capture of Jerusalem in 589 B.C. and the exile in Babylon, it became necessary to re-evaluate the meaning of the covenant.[18]

Some of the people began to look for a national dynasty of the future; others interpreted the covenant of promise as being spiritual. The prophets declared it to be spiritual, and the New Testament apostles explained it as so; however, even with that clear testimony, many still miss the interpretation today. This Davidic line pointed to the Messiah who was to come. The prophet Jeremiah spoke of the day of the New Covenant when the law of God would be written on man's heart.

> *This is the covenant I will make with the house of Israel after that time," declares the LORD. "I will put my law in their minds and write it on their hearts. I will be their God, and they will be my people.* (Jeremiah 31:33)

The Bible is about God's promise of His Son to a fallen people in order to reveal His power and glory in all of His creation. The promise was given through several covenants, but they all point toward the New Covenant in Christ. On this subject Gentry writes;

---

18 L.D. Johnson, *An Introduction Of The Bible*, (Nashville, TN: Convention Press, 1969), 4.

Interestingly, Ezekiel combines the Abrahamic, Mosaic, and Davidic Covenants in the chapters in which he deals with the New Covenant:

My servant David will be king over them, [Davidic] and they will all have one shepherd. They will follow my laws and be careful to keep my decrees [Mosaic]. They will live in the land I gave to my servant Jacob, the land where your fathers lived [Abrahamic]. They and their children and their children's children will live there forever, and David my servant will be their prince forever [Davidic]. I will make a covenant of peace with them; it will be an everlasting covenant. I will establish them and increase their numbers, and I will put my sanctuary among them forever. (Ezekiel 37:24-26)[19]

There is one continuous promise fulfilled in Jesus, the Messiah. Wayne Grudem's *Systematic Theology*, concurs, "The covenant promises to Abraham remained in force as they found fulfillment in Christ."[20] He is the promised seed of the woman and the promised seed of Abraham. He is the prophet after the order of Moses and the son of David (Deuteronomy 18:15). The continuous promise is the story of the Bible.

The Bible was written over a period of 1600 years, with more than 40 authors, 39 books in the Old Covenant and 27 in the New Covenant, yet it is one complete message from God with continuity. It reveals God's heart to have a family and be as one in a relationship with His people. One author says it this way, "What we find in the Bible is not an accumulation of data about God, but rather a living God in a living relationship with living people."[21]

19 Kenneth L. Gentry Jr., *He Shall Have Dominion* (Tyler, TX: Institute for Christian Economics, 1992), 113.
20 Wayne Grudem, *Systematic Theology, An Introduction to Biblical Doctrine* (Grand Rapids, MI: Zondervan Publishing House, 1994), 521.
21 Robert McAfee Brown, *The Bible Speaks to You* (Philadelphia, PA: Westminster Press, 1966), 41.

Application

1. What is a better word for testament?

   _____

2. A covenant may be defined as . . .

   _____

   _____

   _____

3. There are several times that covenants were made by God with individuals, but there was only one _____.

4. Explain the seed of Abraham and give the New Testament verse.

   _____

   _____

   _____

5. After King David, the covenant was linked with him and his descendants. When this line ended in the capture of Jerusalem, the prophets declared a future fulfillment. The Davidic covenant pointed to the _____ who was to come. According to the prophets like Jeremiah, this was the day of the _____.

6. Who is the promised seed of the woman, the promised seed of Abraham, the prophet after the order of Moses, and the son of David?

   _____

7. Begin working on this week's memory verse found in the appendix.

The Authority of God's Word

As a Christian, you have come to believe that the Bible is the Word of God and the eternal source of truth. That is the foundation of your faith. As a believer, you have accepted it as God's Word and your highest authority. It is your rule of faith and conduct. With other religions claiming to have books that are the word of God, how can you be sure? What foundation is present for such confidence in the Bible? This lesson will address the authority of the Bible in your life.

The Word of God Revealed

The Bible reveals to us the wisdom and purpose of God. Revelation means disclosure. God gives us insight into what He has done, and why He has done it. In the Bible, we find out who God is, what His character is like, and what His will and purposes are for humanity. It is in the Bible where we discover God's standard of conduct for society and ourselves. Without a written standard, man would continually adjust his moral beliefs to fit his behavior; therefore, God has given us an established measuring line for conduct.

Beginning with the Books of Moses, which are the first five books of the Old Testament, and continuing through the Books of the Prophets, the plan of God is revealed to us. The culmination of God's revelation is brought forth by sending His own Son, Jesus, as the Word made flesh.

> *In the past, God spoke to our forefathers through the prophets at many times and in various ways, but in these last days, He has spoken to us by His Son, whom He appointed heir of all things, and through whom He made the universe. The Son is the radiance of God's glory and the exact representation of His being, sustaining all things by his powerful word. . .* (Hebrews 1:1-3)

Christ came in the living flesh to reveal what God is like. The God of the Old Testament is the same God of the New Testament. Jesus reveals to us the Father. God is a spirit, and to reveal Himself, He chose to give us a written record and a Living Word. Christ is the Living Word.

> *In the beginning was the Word, and the Word was with God, and the Word was God. The Word became flesh and made His dwelling among us. We have seen His glory, the glory of the One and Only, who came from the Father, full of grace and truth.* (John 1:1, 14)

Christ's coming proved the validity of the prophets and the fulfillment of what they had declared through the ages.

The Word of God Inspired

Inspiration means "God-breathed." It is important for you to see that not only is the Word of God revealed to us, but His Word also has authority through inspiration. While revelation is the truth of God disclosed concerning His relationship with mankind, inspiration is the impulse to preserve the Word handed down through the centuries as God's infallible truth. Both revelation and inspiration are needed. *The Layman's Bible Commentary* explains, "For without revelation, there would be no point in inspiration. Without inspiration, on the other hand, revelation would die with the first person to whom it came."[22]

Inspiration means the Bible is the Word of God given to men as they were moved upon by the Holy Spirit to write it. Every word they wrote was guided and influenced by God. They were not automatic transcribers, rather they wrote using their personalities, yet breathed upon by God Himself. Peter explains,

> *Above all, you must understand that no prophecy of Scripture came about by the prophet's own interpretation. For prophecy never had its origin in the will of man, but men spoke from God as they were carried along by the Holy Spirit.* (2 Peter 1:20, 21)

Paul affirmed this concept by declaring, "All scripture is God-breathed" (2 Timothy 1:16). Though men wrote the Bible, it involved a partnership with God; thus the Bible is like Jesus, the Living Word, both human and divine.

The Word of God Infallible and Inerrant

To say the Bible is infallible and inerrant is to declare that it is error free, absolutely trustworthy as a guide of faith and conduct, and all its teachings are perfect and true. Charles Ford, in his book *The Inspired Scriptures*, writes, "While infallibility emphasizes the trustworthiness of Scripture, inerrancy emphasizes the truthfulness of Scripture."[23] God cannot lie, and our confidence in the Bible is based on the truthfulness of God (Titus 1:2). Many other religions regard their sacred writings as God's Word, yet the writings are what their prophets have said or what their sacred leaders have taught. More than 3,800[24] times the writers in the Old Testament begin their statements with, "The Lord spoke," "the Lord said," or "the Word of the Lord came." It is not sufficient to say the Bible contains the Word of God; rather, it is the Word of God.

Jesus, as the Son of God, believed the Old Testament to be trustworthy. He often spoke about Himself saying, "The Scriptures must be fulfilled" (Mark 14:49). After the resurrection, Jesus appeared to two men on the road to Emmaus. He began with Moses and the Prophets and explained what was in all the Scriptures concerning Himself (Luke 24:27). Time and time again the apostles in the New Testament quoted from the Old to give the meaning of its fulfillment (Romans 16:25, 26).

---

22 *The Layman's Bible Commentary* (Richmond: John Knox Press, 1959), 1, 21.
23 Charles Ford, *The Inspired Scriptures* (Springfield, MO: Gospel Publishing House, 1978), 43.
24 According to Evans, *Great Doctrines of the Bible*, 203.

The Word of God Unified

The Bible was written by 40 different authors from a variety of places, in diverse circumstances, and over an extended period, yet there is perfect unity through the books. There is no disagreement in all of the books of the Bible. Henry Thiessen writes, "These books have one doctrinal viewpoint, one moral standard, one plan of salvation, one program of the ages, and one worldview."[25]

Occasionally someone will claim the Bible has contradictions. Often quoted are the Gospels that give a variety of views of the same accounts. Upon closer observation, they are not contradictions at all, rather one writer gives certain points and another includes details. Compare this to eyewitnesses at an automobile accident, each describes the same event, but different items may be contained in the description that the others left out yet without contradictions.

As a Christian, you can count on the Word of God as the final authority in every area of your life. It is the Supreme Court on all matters. It tells you how to conduct your life, along with God's plan and purpose. It gives you the proper worldview and principles from which to make decisions. You can read the Bible with total confidence knowing that every word is true and trustworthy. As a disciple, your goal should be to submit fully to the authority of God's Word and allow the Holy Spirit to bring illumination of the Word.

---

25 Henry Clarence Thiessen, *Introduction to the New Testament* (Grand Rapids, MI: WM. B. Eerdmans Publishing Company, 1943), 86.

Application

1. What does revelation mean?

   _____

2. What we find in the Bible is not an accumulation of data about God, but rather a _____
   God in _____ relationship with _____ people.

3. What is the culmination of the revelation of God?

   _____

   _____

4. What does inspiration mean?

   _____

5. What does the Bible mean when it says that men spoke from God as the Holy Spirit carried them along?

   _____

   _____

   _____

6. What does it mean to say the Bible is infallible and inerrant?

   _____

   _____

7. Inerrancy emphasizes the _____ of Scripture.

8. How many times in the Old Testament did the writers introduce their statements with, "The Lord said…"? _____

9. Why is it not sufficient to say the Bible contains the Word of God?

   _____

10. The books of the Bible have one _____ viewpoint, one _____
    standard, one plan of _____, one program of the ages, and one _____.

Handling God's Word

Christians want to know how to improve their understanding of the Bible and receive the blessings from it as a living book. Both of these considerations should be our goal when approaching the Bible. Studying the Bible brings you to a better appreciation and understanding of the Scriptures, while the devotional approach serves as your spiritual food for strength.

Devotional Reading

In your spiritual growth, daily devotional reading is to you what food is in your physical health. There is no substitute for regular times with God and His Word.

Your spirit needs to be fed. Head knowledge, though important, is not enough. Knowledge alone can produce pride (1 Corinthians 8:1). Christians can grow cold in their Christian walk just studying the Bible as a textbook. That is why you must meditate on the Word of God. The Word of God is the bread of life. The Bible tells us that Jesus is our manna (John 6:31-35). He is the Living Word. When God provided manna for the Children of Israel in the wilderness, they had to gather the manna each day. When you approach the Bible to hear from the Lord, you are eating this manna. Jesus said, "If you remain in me and my words remain in you, ask whatever you wish, and it will be done for you" (John 15:7). We must have God's Word living in us. When being tempted by the devil, Jesus responded by saying, "It is written: 'Man does not live by bread alone, but on every word that comes from the mouth of God'" (Matthew 4:4).

Devotional reading does not have to be lengthy. A chapter at a time can be adequate. Begin with a prayer asking the Holy Spirit to illuminate the verses to you. It is helpful to read the same passage several times praying and thinking about the verses each time. Place yourself in the text. Ask yourself what you would be thinking, feeling, hearing, and doing if you were there in the pages of the Bible. Ask, "What is God saying to me today through these verses?" Be prepared to write down what you receive from your meditations.

Try using the one thought method. Robert Clinton in his book *Having a Ministry That Lasts* introduces this method. He explains, "The one thought method is a process used by an individual during quiet time in which that person reads a portion of Scripture and from his thoughts about it, selects one, writes it down, turns it into a prayer, and prays it back to God."[26] It is important in this devotional

---

26 J. Robert Clinton, *Having a Ministry That Lasts* (Altadena, CA: Barnabas Publishers, 1997), 86.

exercise not to turn these thoughts into an application for others rather than yourself. Instead of what others should do, say, "I must . . ." Make these times personal meditation.

Some portions of the Bible may fit into devotional reading better than others. For example, the genealogies and ceremonial laws in the Old Testament are better for study than devotions. The Gospels will be helpful, particularly John, as you are learning to meditate. The stories of miracles and the powerful workings of Christ can help to build your faith. The Book of Acts is also very helpful in this area. All of the Epistles, Psalms, and Proverbs are perfect for meditation. As you grow in your devotional life, you will want to travel through the entire Old Testament and New Testament.

There are many devotional guides available. Some are beneficial and thought-provoking; however, a word of caution is in order concerning devotional guides. Some may have very little of the Word of God. A kind story about what Christians should do, while it may be refreshing, it is not the Word of God. If you use a devotional guide, do not let it replace your time in the actual Scriptures. It is better to meditate a few verses and write out your thoughts and prayer than to read several pages of what others have written.

Have a pen, highlighter, and paper with you during your devotions. You may want to mark thoughts alongside certain Bible verse or underline them for emphasis. It is a good practice to date your notes both in your Bible and in your notebook. It is rewarding to look back at your notes.

Studious Reading

True disciples will have a hunger to study the Bible beyond devotional reading. It is important to study your Bible if you are going to answer questions, share your faith, or disciple others. Paul gave Timothy a command to study saying, "Do your best to present yourself to God as one approved, a workman who does not need to be ashamed and who correctly handles the word of truth" (2 Timothy 2:15).

Reading is a must for disciples. If you do not like to read, pray and ask the Holy Spirit to change that in you. By reading His Word, you will begin to develop a desire for reading. If God thinks it is important enough to put His Word in print, we should value reading. Paul valued reading the Scriptures and books very highly. He once wrote to Timothy, "When you come, bring the cloak that I left with Carpus at Troas, and my scrolls, especially the parchments" (2 Timothy 4:13). The scrolls were his books, and the parchments were the Scriptures. He treasured them greatly. On the eve of his martyrdom, he wanted these books and writings to possibly be given to the faithful for their preservation.

Methods

Some good Bible study methods include discovering the central theme of the verses or chapters and discovering how the theme is developed with its historical background. That is a valuable system but may seem overwhelming for a beginner. A better method is what I call a Devotional Study Method. It takes your devotional reading one step further by studying the same material you are meditating upon. For example, if you are meditating through the Book of Ephesians, you might first read half of a chapter per day during your devotional time using the one thought method. Then, after your devotional time, discover more about the actual chapter. (1) What is the leading subject? (2) What lesson can be learned from this chapter? (3) What verse(s) stood out in that chapter? (4) What does this chapter teach about Christ? (5) Is there a warning for Christians? (6) Is there a word of encouragement? (7) Is there a duty to carry out? (8) Does it give a promise? (9) Is there a prayer that can be echoed? (10) Is there something in the chapter that was hard to understand? Write out your responses to any of the ten questions that apply to that chapter study.

Tools for Study

1. A study Bible—You may want a Bible that you can write in.

2. Bible Dictionary[27]—This will help define certain words.

3. Concordance[28]—Words in the Bible are listed alphabetically along with the chapter and verse.

4. Today there are many Bible study helps online. You can search quickly on the internet to find Bible study helps free of charge.

5. Notebook and pen—Keep your notes for later perusing.

6. A quiet place—A table or writing surface will help.

---

27 Vines *Bible* Dictionary, Ungers *Bible* Dictionary, or Nelson's *Bible* Dictionary
28 Strong's Concordance or Young's Concordance

Application

1. In your spiritual growth, daily devotional reading is to you what _____ is to you in your _____ growth.

2. You should begin with _____, asking the Holy Spirit to illuminate the scriptures to you.

3. Explain the one-thought method.

_____

_____

_____

4. What is one caution concerning devotional guides?

_____

_____

5. What is your greatest hindrance to regular devotional reading?

_____

_____

6. In your own words, write out the verse in which Paul tells Timothy to learn to handle the Word of truth.

_____

_____

_____

7. Why is reading a must for disciples?

_____

_____

_____

Interpreting God's Word

A question new converts often ask is why there are so many different interpretations of Scripture? It may be frustrating to find that there are a variety of views on what the Bible means in particular passages. How do you know what is right? And how do you have confidence in the interpretation that you have received? These are valid questions. Wrestling with these concepts is a sign of maturity. The purpose of this lesson is to give principles to guide you in your Bible study.

Who Is Right?

"Why didn't God make it clearer for us?" That question has been asked many times. First of all, in the whole scope of things, the essential matters are clear and easy to understand. Most of the Bible is clear in its message. Controversies hardly ever arise in the majority of the cases. As a general rule, the Church as a whole agrees on the majors.

Second, because we are mere men, it is possible to misinterpret the Scriptures. That is why we need the Holy Spirit to illuminate the wonders of God to our finite minds. Third, though the Bible is fully current and applicable to our day, the original recipients of the Scriptures lived in a different culture and time. A study that helps reveal Bible customs and manners will shed some light on some difficult passages; however, we need principles by which to interpret.

A teachable and non-defensive attitude goes a long way in "rightly dividing the Word of truth." Once a position is chosen on a particular subject, one must guard against pride lest that becomes a hindrance to understanding something differently. Some people take pride in not ever changing their views on a matter. While consistency and faithfulness to truth is a virtue, one must be cautious about becoming unteachable. The Bible tells us about a man named Apollos who had a thorough knowledge of the Scriptures, yet he demonstrated a teachable heart.

> *Meanwhile a Jew named Apollos, a native of Alexandria, came to Ephesus. He was a learned man, with a thorough knowledge of the Scriptures. He had been instructed in the way of the Lord, and he spoke with great fervor and taught about Jesus accurately, though he knew only the baptism of John. He began to speak boldly in the synagogue. When Priscilla and Aquila heard him, they invited him to their home and explained to him the way of God more adequately.* (Acts 18:24-26)

Later on, in the letter to the Corinthians, Paul identified Apollos as an apostle who labored with him. He used himself and Apollos as an example of not going beyond what is written, which is a key to correct interpretation of the Scriptures.

> *Now, brothers, I have applied these things to myself and Apollos for your benefit, so that you may learn from us the meaning of the saying, "Do not go beyond what is written." Then you will not take pride in one man over against another.* (1 Corinthians 4:6)

Principles of Interpretation

To maintain integrity in interpreting the scriptures, we should follow certain principles. This avoids personal application of meaning and helps to guard against strong presuppositions. It takes discipline to hold to these principles when they fly in the face of our preconceptions.

Hermeneutics is the study of the methodological principles of interpretation of the Bible. There are four principles of interpreting Scripture that will be tremendously helpful in keeping a serious Bible student on track.

Comparative Revelation: This order of interpretation allows the scripture to interpret the scripture. It is called biblical hermeneutics. High confidence can be attributed to this type of interpretation. Interpret the Bible in light of the Bible. When we allow the New Testament apostles to tell us the meaning of Old Testament prophets, we have discovered the foundation of the church. Though I believe apostles and prophets still exist in the church today, I think the meaning of Ephesians 2:19-22 is most fully explained in the light of the church being built upon the foundation of the New Testament apostles and the Old Testament prophets. The words of the Old Testament prophets are interpreted by the New Testament apostles, ". . . you are . . . of the household of God, having been built on the foundation of the apostles and prophets, Jesus Christ Himself being the chief corner stone, in whom the whole building, being joined together, grows into a holy temple in the Lord, in whom you also are being built together for a dwelling place of God in the Spirit." (Emphasis mine.)

Contextual Revelation: Interpret the scriptures in light of the context. This principle is regularly overlooked. Too often verses are taken out of context and made to mean something entirely different. This means of interpretation should always be practiced. There may be allegorical benefits to scriptures, but the context is the authority for interpretation.

Clear Revelation: Interpret the difficult passages in light of the clear passages. This is similar to biblical hermeneutics. We include this principle, however, to keep the meanings interpreted in light of already readily accepted revelation. Do not do the opposite and try to understand the clear passages by the complex ones.

Comprehensive Revelation: Interpret scriptures within the scope of the whole counsel of God. Scriptures, even in context, still need to be placed within the wider view. This prevents doctrine from being built upon isolated passages. The overall theme of God's purposes and plan gives stability in interpretations. The Bible gives us the master plan of God for the ages.

By following these four principles of interpretation, you can have confidence that you are on solid ground and have a reason for your approach.

Application

1. Give three reasons why Scriptures may not be clear to understand.

_____

_____

_____

_____

2. Explain each of the four principles of interpretation.

    1) Comparative Revelation

    _____

    _____

    _____

    2) Contextual Revelation

    _____

    _____

    _____

    3) Clear Revelation

    _____

    _____

    _____

    4) Comprehensive Revelation

    _____

    _____

    _____

Growing in God's Word

When we were children, we sang a song in children's church that said, "Read your Bible and pray every day, and you will grow, grow, grow." With body actions emphasizing the growing part, we would squat down and pretend that we were growing a little each time we said, "grow." In today's lesson, you are reminded of the benefits of God's Word and growth in your life. Peter instructs us to crave spiritual milk like babies who must have it. He writes, "Like newborn babies, crave pure spiritual milk, so that by it you may grow up in your salvation" (1 Peter 2:2). He calls the Word of God "pure spiritual milk." We must consume the Word of God regularly to grow spiritually.

The Workings of His Word

Paul tells the Thessalonians that the Word of God was at work in them (1 Thessalonians 2:13). The word was at work in them because they accepted it as God's Word. When you cherish the Word of God and apply it to your life, there are special benefits.

God's Word Brings Salvation

> *For you have been born again, not of perishable seed, but of imperishable, through the living and enduring Word of God.* (1 Peter 1:23)

Peter says that we are born again through the living Word of God that remains forever and will never change. The Word of God is the means by which a man receives the incorruptible seed (Ephesians 1:13).

God's Word Brings Faith

> *Consequently, faith comes from hearing the message, and the message is heard through the word of Christ.* (Romans 10:17)

Faith comes when you hear the message of Christ. Preaching the Gospel is the ordinary means of salvation. When a person hears the Word personally, it is a spiritual hearing, and it brings faith and is a Living Word for him. When faith comes, an individual can see a portion of what God sees. That is called faith. God's kind of faith. If you are aware of lacking faith, the best thing to do is to find out what God's Word says about the matter. Read, pray, and meditate those verses that apply to your situation. God will bring faith to your heart as you apply the Word of God. Be patient; that is how faith comes.

God's Word Brings Transformation

Therefore, get rid of all moral filth and the evil that is so prevalent and humbly accept the word planted in you, which can save you. (James 1:21)

The Word of God engrafted, or applied to your souls (which is your mind, will, and emotions), has the power to transform your soul. The word "you" is often translated as "soul" from the Greek word *psuche*. Your soul is transformed by renovating your mind. Paul writes to the Roman Christians, "Do not be conformed to the pattern of this world but be transformed by the renewing of your mind" (Romans 12:2).

God's Word Brings Cleansing

You are already clean because of the word I have spoken to you. (John 15:3)

Paul speaks of the Church and says we are cleansed by the washing of the water by the Word (Ephesians 5:26). It has the power to cleanse our thought life, attitudes, and emotions. In the Psalms, David said that a man can stay pure by living according to the Word of God (Psalm 119:9).

God's Word Brings Clarity

For the Word of God is living and active. Sharper than any double-edged sword, it penetrates even to dividing soul and spirit, joints and marrow; it judges the thoughts and attitudes of the heart. (Hebrews 4:12)

We need a standard beyond our feelings and emotions. We must depend upon the Word, which is able to divide between our soul and spirit. Your mind, your will, and your emotions might be telling you to do something that is contrary to the will of God. Confusion will enter into your life unless you see God's Word on the matter. Once you receive God's Word, the matter is closed. The Word is the final authority. It doesn't matter how you feel or what your intentions are, the Word is able to judge your heart properly. You cannot clearly judge your own heart (1 Corinthians 4:1). The Word of God and the Lord can judge you. The Word can point out to you what you need to see. The entrance of God's Word gives light and understanding (Psalm 119:130).

God's Word Brings Hope

For everything that was written in the past was written to teach us, so that through endurance and the encouragement of the Scriptures we might have hope. (Romans 15:4)

Hope is what keeps your soul secure (Hebrews 6:19). You lose hope when you fail to remember what God has to say about the situation. Regular time in God's Word will keep you emotional and mentally steadfast.

God's Word Brings Strength

Now I commit you to God and to the word of his grace, which can build you up and give you an inheritance among all those who are sanctified. (Acts 20:32)

Jesus said that anyone who hears His words and puts them to practice is like a man building a house, who dug down deep and laid the foundation on a rock. When a flood came, the torrent struck that house but could not shake it because it was well built (Luke 6:47-48). Your life will be settled and strengthened in proportion to your willingness to hear and practice God's Word.

Putting the Word of God into practice in your life is being a "doer of the Word." James tells us that if we do not continue in the Word of God, we will be like one who looks into the mirror and goes away forgetting what he looks like (James 1:22-25). By spending time reading, meditating, memorizing, and studying God's Word, you are gazing into God's mirror. That is when it will benefit you the most and bring blessings into your life. Paul told Timothy to continue in "what you have learned" (2 Timothy 3:14, 15). Your spiritual life will persevere to maturity by continuing in the Word of God.

Application

1. What does Peter call the Word of God?

_____

2. Explain the seven benefits of the Word of God working in you. Give an explanation of how each works.

   1) God's Word brings salvation.

   _____

   _____

   2) God's Word brings faith.

   _____

   _____

   3) God's Word brings transformation.

   _____

   _____

   4) God's Word brings cleansing.

   _____

   _____

   5) God's Word brings clarity.

   _____

   _____

   6) God's Word brings hope.

   _____

   _____

   7) God's Word brings strength.

   _____

   _____

Overc

A major key to spiritu
ciples who remain ste
their lives. The very e
wrote to the Christi
events as the theme

> *Everyone who*
> *will not last,*
> *someone run*
> *make it my*
> *prize. (1 Co*

The Amplified
saying that he
test. Paul taugh
learn spiritual
yourself to be godly" (1 Timotny ...,

The following rotated text (sidebar):

Spiritual disciplines should not be seen as "willpower," but rather
The essence of spiritual disciplines rests upon His life in us da
itual disciplines include learning to live our lives like Jesus
selves to Him. It is the discipline of allowing Christ to
us up to hear and receive His life more clearly. It doe
but rather, one who is separated unto life in Chris

Spiritual disciplines are for normal Christia
he writes, "God intends the disciplines o
who have jobs, who care for children
best exercised in the midst of our rel
friends and neighbors."[31]

The Disciplines

Other spiritual disc
to Dallas Willard'

Disciplines

What Are Spiritual Disciplines?

Robert Clinton, in his book *Clinton Biblical Leadership Commentary*, defines spiritual disciplines, "Spiritual disciplines are activities of mind and body purposefully undertaken to bring personality and total being into effective cooperation with the Spirit of God so as to reflect Kingdom life."[29]

Richard Foster in his book *Celebration of Discipline*, clarifies how spiritual disciplines serve us. He explains, "By themselves spiritual disciplines can do nothing; they can only get us to the place where something can be done. They are God's means of grace. The inner righteousness we seek is not something that is poured on our heads. God has ordained the disciplines of the spiritual life as the means by which we place ourselves where he can bless us."[30]

29 J. Robert Clinton, *Clinton's Biblical Leadership Commentary* (Altadena, CA: Barnabas Publishers, 1999), 615.
30 Richard Foster, *Celebration of Discipline, The Path to Spiritual Growth* (New York, NY: HarperCollins Publishers, 1978), 7.

the surrender of our rights to Christ.

...ly, not just in occasional decisions. Spir-

...by giving our time, energies, and our total

...ve His life through us. These disciplines open

...not mean one is separated from life as a recluse,

...s, not spiritual giants. Foster makes a great point when

...the spiritual life to be for ordinary human beings: people

...who wash dishes and mow lawns. In fact, the disciplines are

...ationships with our husband or wife, our brothers and sisters, our

...plines could be added to the following list; however, I have chosen to use and add

...s list from his book, *The Spirit of the Disciplines*.

...of Engagement

Study—diligently studying the Word of God.

- **Meditation**—to thoughtfully and thoroughly consider the Word of God to clearly hear and obey His Word.

- **Prayer**—practicing communing with and petitioning God.

- **Worship**—to ascribe God's greatness and holiness as centered in Christ. This practice is done alone as well with God's people.

- **Celebration**—to come together with others to eat and drink, to sing and dance, and to relate stories of God's mighty works in our lives.

- **Service**—to give your energy and goods to help others. This discipline is especially important to those who have influence.

- **Fellowship**—to engage in the common life of the Church with other disciples by sharing and receiving of the spiritual gifts with each other.

- **Confession**—to bear one's soul and faults to those who can be trusted. This discipline removes burdens and helps to avoid sins as well as brings healing.

---

31 Ibid., 1.

- **Submission**—the highest level of Christian community involving humility, brokenness, trust, honesty, transparency, and at times repentance and restitution. This preserves peace and unity.

- **Giving**—the practice of honoring God with substance. This includes tithes, offerings, and giving to those in need.

Disciplines of Abstinence

- **Solitude**—having time alone during the day, week, or occasionally getting away from others to spend time with God by yourself. It causes you to confront your own soul. Jesus often got alone.

- **Silence**—to close yourself off from sounds or noise whether it is music, words, or other distractions. To refrain from turning on the TV, radio, media, or other distractions may be difficult at first, but necessary in times of listening to God.

- **Fasting**—abstaining from natural food to feast on God. This includes water for short times, less than three days. Fasting can include one meal, an entire day, or extended times without food. A partial fast is abstaining from tasty foods and eating or drinking only what is necessary for strength.

- **Frugality**—abstain from using money or goods at your disposal to merely satisfy desires for attention or status. This discipline helps to keep priorities in line.

- **Chastity**—Robert Clinton says chastity is, "manifesting the qualities of sexual wholeness and integrity in relationship to oneself, to persons of the same sex, and to persons of the opposite sex. Learn to value highly your own personhood and sexuality. Guard your thought life. Abstain from any form of entertainment which might indulge improper sexual thoughts. Deliberately develop positive relationships with those of the opposite sex which are healthy and do not focus on sexuality. Don't allow yourself to be put in potentially compromising situations with an individual of the opposite sex."[32]

- **Secrecy**—to practice not divulging or discussing to others your good deeds or accomplishments. Allow God to vindicate you and be your promoter. This brings great strength, trust, and confidence in God.

- **Sacrifice**—to give to others out of your own need. This heightens your awareness that God is your source.

This week we will address some of the above disciplines in more detail. By practicing these spiritual disciplines, you will discover the joy of placing Christ first in every area of your life. His life flows out of us.

---

32 J. Robert Clinton, *Clinton's Biblical Leadership Commentary* (Altadena, CA: Barnabas Publishers, 1999), 616-618.

Application

1. The very essence of the word _____ comes from being disciplined.

2. Write out in your own words what Paul told Timothy concerning spiritual disciplines in 1 Timothy 4:7.

    _____

    _____

    _____

3. Which disciplines of engagement are needed most in your life? Check as many as apply.

    - Study
    - Meditation
    - Prayer
    - Worship
    - Celebration
    - Service
    - Fellowship
    - Confession
    - Submission
    - Giving

4. Which disciplines of abstinence are needed most in your life? Check as many as apply.

    - Solitude
    - Silence
    - Fasting
    - Frugality
    - Chastity
    - Secrecy
    - Sacrifice

5. Explain one discipline of abstinence in your own words.

    _____

    _____

    _____

Discipline of Prayer

There are three spiritual disciplines that Jesus spoke about in Matthew 6, in which He apparently expects us to participate: prayer, fasting, and giving. He says the same thing for each discipline, "When you give, when you pray, or when you fast." He does not indicate how often, but He does not say "if." He assumes that a follower of His would practice all three. Prayer is one of the essential disciplines in the life of a disciple. It is considered most central because prayer is communion with God. All other disciplines cannot be practiced without it. Fasting is only a hunger strike without it; meditation and all other spiritual disciplines are unfruitful without it. Therefore, prayer is not optional for the growing Christian.

What Is Prayer?

Prayer is communion with God, nothing less and nothing more. It is nothing less, or it becomes a repetition of words, acts of religion, and meaningless chants. It is nothing more because what could be greater than communing with God. Effective prayer is more than an occasional outburst of feelings or an outflow of petitions; it is a life positioned before God. A prayer life is being led by the Holy Spirit and committed to participating with God to see His will done on earth. Prayer then becomes the spoken words, heartfelt thoughts, and earnest desires placed in the individual's life by God Himself and prayed heavenward by the prayer.

Participating in Prayer

There is no greater classroom for learning to pray than a prayer closet. The best way to learn to pray is to get alone with God. If prayer is communing with God, then it becomes a natural thing when a person is shut in with Him. There is no reason to make prayer complicated or for the newest Christian to think he cannot participate. Prayer develops in the life of a believer as the Christian himself grows. Prayer and spiritual growth go hand in hand. You cannot pray without growing, for prayer is being in touch with Him who has all wisdom and knowledge. The lack of earnestness to pray and the emptiness of spirituality are quickly discovered when one is locked into a time of prayer. The cry of a prayerless soul and the restlessness of a carnal mind will drive one from the prayer room until discipline turns into delight. It is while you are before God that He can to lead you into prayer. A person of prayer will also find thanksgiving, praise, and worship coming from his heart throughout the day. Prayer becomes a lifestyle in thought and words, yet nothing can build a prayer life like spending time alone with God.

The secret to prayer is spending time with God. It is not by the clock or the amount of recorded time that you pray, but personal time alone with God. Those who have served exemplary lives in Christ have all been people of prayer, often spending hours a day praying. Most rose early to spend time in prayer before the day began and then another time of prayer before the day had finished. E. M Bounds quotes Martin Luther in his book, *Power to Prayer*, "If I fail to spend two hours in prayer each morning, the Devil gets the victory through the day. I have so much business I cannot get on without spending three hours daily in prayer."[33]

Jesus is our example in prayer. He often spent the night in prayer or arose for prayer while it was still dark (Luke 6:12). The Bible tells us that Paul prayed both night and day (1 Thessalonians 3:10). To be a person of prayer one must give time to pray. Bounds, writes, "No man can do a great and enduring work for God who is not a man of prayer, and no man can be a man of prayer who does not give much time to praying."[34]

God has chosen prayer as one of His means of grace to accomplish His will. In the same way He has chosen preaching to bring forth the Gospel that men might be saved; He has selected prayer as one of His instruments. That is why a true disciple of Christ must be a person of prayer. To participate in prayer is to submit your life unto God. Out of that relationship with Him, your life can become one of His means of His work.

Power of Prayer

Prayer is not intended to alter God's course; it is a means for us to participate with God's purposes. Therefore, prayer is powerful. When we become His instrument of work in the spiritual exercise of prayer, we join with God's will to see His mighty power performed. John, the apostle, writes,

> *Now, this is the confidence that we have in Him, that if we ask anything according to His will, He hears us. And if we know that He hears us, whatever we ask, we know that we have the petitions that we have asked of Him.* (I John 5:14, 15)

The power of prayer is expressed in R. A Torrey's quote, "All that God is, and all that God has, is at the disposal of prayer. But we must use the key. Prayer can do anything that God can do, and as God can do anything, prayer is omnipotent."[35] The Book of James tells us the earnest prayer of a righteous man has great power and wonderful results (James 5:16). Power and life spring from the praying church as though it was the womb of God. We are the temple of the Holy Spirit, and the river of life flows through praying people.

---

33 E.M. Bounds, *Power Through Prayer* (Chicago, IL: Moody Press, 1979), 54-55.
34 Ibid., 59.
35 R. A. Torrey, *The Power of Prayer* (Grand Rapids, MI: Zondervan Publishing House, 1960), 17.

We read in the Book of Revelation that when God wanted to bring forth His judgments and work upon the earth, He used the prayers of the saints. The prayers of the saints are kept as incense before God. An angel took fire off the altar in heaven and mixed it with the prayers of the saints and threw it to the earth. Then judgments took place upon those who opposed God and persecuted the saints (Revelation 8:3-5). This is a picture of how God has chosen to use the prayers of the saints to perform His work. He takes our prayers and mixes them with His power to bring forth His will. A disciple must not disregard the power of prayer.

Persevering in Prayer

Persistence in prayer is a key to a successful prayer life. This is not only for what it does for you, but the result of answered prayer is a great motivator to pray. When teaching His disciples about prayer, Jesus uses an illustration of a persistent friend who comes at midnight to make a request. He declared,

> *"I tell you, though he will not get up and give him the bread because he is his friend, yet because of the man's boldness he will get up and give him as much as he needs. So I say to you: Ask and it will be given to you; seek and you will find; knock and the door will be opened to you."* (Luke 11:8, 9)

That is not a repetition of prayer in unbelief, but it is persevering in faith to what God has promised. Paul, the apostle, tells us to be faithful in prayer, constant in prayer, devoted to prayer, and to pray without ceasing.

Dick Eastman tells the story of George Muller, a 19th-century prayer warrior and man of God, who was known for his prayer life. He said that once Muller was persuaded that a thing was right, he went on praying for it until the end comes. He once said, "'The great point is never to give up until the answer comes. I have been praying for sixty-three years and eight months for one man's conversion. He is not saved yet, but he will be. How can it be otherwise. . . I am praying.' The day came when Muller's friend received Christ. It did not come until Muller's casket was lowered in the ground. There, near an open grave, this friend gave his heart to God. Prayers of perseverance had won another battle. Muller's success may be summarized in four powerful words: He did not quit."[36] May that be said of you as a disciple that you never quit in prayer.

---

36 Dick Eastman, *No Easy Road* (Grand Rapids: Baker Book House, 1971), 96-97.

Application

1. Define prayer.

   _____

   _____

2. The best way to learn to pray is to _____.

3. What is quickly discovered when a person shuts himself or herself up for a time of prayer?

   _____

   _____

4. What is the secret to successful prayer?

   _____

   _____

5. God has chosen prayer as one of His _____ to accomplish His will.

6. Write out 1 John 5:14, 15. Write in your own words.

   _____

   _____

7. Where does the Bible say that the earnest (fervent) prayer of a righteous man has great power and wonderful results?

   _____

8. Why is persistence in prayer a key to a successful prayer life?

   _____

   _____

9. Paul challenges us to be faithful in prayer, _____ in prayer, devoted to prayer, and to _____ _____ _____.

The Practical Aspects of Prayer

Prayer, like evangelism, is often talked about but participated in very little. There are many books and teachings on how to pray, or how to be effective in your prayer life. While these materials may be very helpful, caution is in order to guard against making prayer complicated. There are no magic formulas for prayer, but there are some principles and practical aspects that all disciples should learn.

Facets of Prayer

When Jesus was asked by His disciples to teach them to pray, He used a model prayer. Jesus' model in Matthew 6:9-13, included seven aspects of prayer.

1. Worship: "Our Father in heaven, hallowed be your name . . ."

2. Submission: "Your kingdom come, your will be done, on earth as it is in heaven . . ."

3. Request: "Give us today our daily bread. . ."

4. Repentance: "Forgive us our sins. . ."

5. Forgiveness: "As we forgive those who sin against us. . ."

6. Resistance: "And lead us not into temptation but deliver us from evil."

7. Thanksgiving: "For it is your power and glory forever."

Jesus gave an outline or guide in which to pray. As beautiful as the Lord's prayer is, it is not intended to be words of repetition but rather a guide to prayer. By using this simple model, we can see the areas that prayer should cover. Since prayer is communicating with God, it is essential that listening be a part of each portion. For example, while you are worshipping and giving honor and adoration to the Father, it would be to your advantage to pause and listen in your spirit to see if the Holy Spirit gives you a strong impression or spiritual thought. It is also helpful to be prepared to write down what you receive in prayer.[37]

---

37 By writing down your thoughts you can draw upon them later, share them with friends and check them against what the Bible has to say. Remember, the Scriptures are our highest authority.

ACTS of Prayer

There is a four-part, easy-to-remember approach to prayer that has been designated as the "ACTS of Prayer." It mirrors Jesus' model. Not only does it speak of the practice of prayer itself, but it also gives a summary of the practices of prayer. It is a time-honored way to remember an effective means of praying by using the acronym ACTS: Adoration, Confession, Thanksgiving, and Supplication.

ADORATION (Worship)—Worship means to kiss or to prostrate oneself in reverence. The true heart of a pray-er is one who approaches God in adoration. Adoration sees God as supreme and magnifies His great name. Jesus said the Father seeks those who worship Him in spirit and in truth (John 4:23, 24). Worship is the highest form of prayer. It is communicating your love and reverence to a Holy God.

CONFESSION (Repentance)—If we confess our sins, God is faithful and just to forgive us of our sins and cleanse us from all unrighteousness (1 John 1:9). To confess means to tell God of your sin with openness and honesty. It is the first outward step of the fruit of repentance. To confess also includes saying what God says about your sin or difficulty.

THANKSGIVING (Gratefulness)—A celebration of thanksgiving enables you to recognize the work of God. It reveals your surrender to His control. Thanksgiving means a proclamation of a job well done. Thanksgiving says to God, "I trust you and you know what is best; therefore, I am grateful for what you have done and wait with anticipation for your good will." The alternative is anger and bitterness toward God. We are told to give thanks in all circumstances because that is God's will for us (1 Thessalonians 5:18).

SUPPLICATION (Petition and Intercession)—Supplication means to make request or entreat. This is when we petition God for a specific request. Intercession on behalf of others may include specific request. Intercession goes beyond specific request with the help of the Holy Spirit when we do not know how we ought to pray. He helps our inabilities through groanings that cannot be uttered (Romans 8:26,27).

Hindrances to Prayer

There are certain elements in the life of a Christian that can hinder prayers. For our prayers to be productive, we should consider these five areas.

1. Prayers can be hindered if you regard known sin in your life. If you regard known sin in your life, that sin will become an idol and take the place of God because of your insistence upon disobedience.

    Psalms 66:18—If I had cherished sin in my heart, the Lord would not have listened.

    Isaiah 59:2—But your iniquities have separated you from your God; your sins have hidden his face from you, so that he will not hear.

    Proverbs 28:9—If anyone turns a deaf ear to the law, even his prayers are detestable.

2. Prayers can be hindered if you asked selfishly.

   James 4:3—When you ask, you do not receive, because you ask with wrong motives, that you may spend what you get on your pleasures.

3. Prayers can be hindered if you pray in unbelief.

   James 1:6-8—But when he asks, he must believe and not doubt, because he who doubts is like a wave of the sea, blown and tossed by the wind. That man should not think he will receive anything from the Lord; he is a double-minded man, unstable in all he does.

4. Prayers can be hindered if one dishonors his spouse.

   1 Peter 3:7—Husbands, in the same way be considerate as you live with your wives, and treat them with respect as the weaker partner and as heirs with you of the gracious gift of life, so that nothing will hinder your prayers.

5. Prayers can be hindered if you leave unresolved conflict.

   Matthew 5:23, 24—Therefore, if you are offering your gift at the altar and there remember that your brother has something against you, leave your gift there in front of the altar. First go and be reconciled to your brother; then come and offer your gift.

God has called you to a service of prayer. The discipline of prayer is most rewarded with answered prayer and time spent with God. When people see their prayers answered, they are motivated to pray. May God reveal to you the vital importance of your life in prayer.

Application

1. List the seven facets of Jesus' prayer model.

   - _____

   - _____

   - _____

   - _____

   - _____

   - _____

   - _____

2. In your own words write out an explanation of the four parts of the "ACTS of Prayer."

   ADORATION

   _____

   _____

   CONFESSION

   _____

   _____

   THANKSGIVING

   _____

   _____

   SUPPLICATION

   _____

   _____

3. Which hindrance to prayer could possible apply to you?

   _____

   _____

   _____

Discipline of Fasting

Jesus tied prayer and fasting together when explaining why the disciples were unable to cast out a demon. He said, "This kind does not go out except through prayer and fasting" (Matthew 17:21 NASV). Fasting is one of the three disciplines that Jesus expected from His followers. He addressed all three in Matthew 6 by saying, "When you give, when you pray, and when you fast."

What Is Fasting?

To fast is to abstain from food, and for short periods even from water, for spiritual purposes. A total or absolute fast includes abstinence from food and water. The Bible does not record such a fast for more than three days except for the supernatural fast of Moses and Elijah. The reason, of course, is that the body cannot go without water for much more than three days. A normal fast involves abstaining from food, whether in solid or liquid form, but not abstaining from water. A partial-fast sometimes called a "Daniel fast," is when a person restricts his diet to only food necessary for strength and does not eat tasty foods. The prophet Daniel went on such a fast for twenty-one days in which he ate no meat or choice food or wine (Daniel 10:3). There are times in which people find themselves in health conditions, suffering from diabetes or other physical disorders in which they may be advised to not go on a total fast or normal fast. That does not prevent them from participating, however; they can enter a partial fast to some degree.

Fasting Under the Old Covenant

In the Old Testament, fasting was ordered only on the Day of Atonement. That was the only time that it was required. It was called a day in which to "deny yourself" or "afflict your soul" (Leviticus 16:29). Fasting in the Old Testament was often related to repentance and humbling oneself before God. After the children of God went into the captivity of Babylon, fasting became more of a merit-based activity. This was not God's kind of fast and the prophet Isaiah spoke against such in the most complete chapter on fasting, Isaiah 58. This merit-based type of fasting continued until the time of Jesus. During the time of Christ, Jews fasted twice a week but with a lot of display and hypocrisy. It was against this backdrop that Jesus corrected their type of fasting.

Fasting in Jesus' Ministry

In Matthew 9, John's disciples came to Jesus and asked Him why they and the Pharisees fasted, but Jesus' disciples did not. Jesus explained that while He was with them, it was not necessary, but after He was gone His disciples would fast. He continued His teaching by explaining that you do not sew a new patch on an old garment because it will shrink and tear the garment worse. He also used the analogy that you do not put new wine into old wineskins, lest it burst and the wine is lost. Jesus was saying that the New Covenant fast was not under the old order of law. Fasting under the New Covenant would have a different emphasis. It is not a time of mourning and repentance, but rather a time to commune with God. His statement that His disciples would fast after He was gone is the strongest support for Christians fasting today.

Besides His teaching in the Sermon on the Mount concerning fasting, Jesus demonstrated His view on fasting by participating in a forty-day, Spirit-led fast Himself. Most scholars believe that Jesus' fast was abstinence from food and not necessarily from water because the scripture says that after forty days He was hungry (Luke 4:2-3). Nothing is said about His thirst. It was also in the area of hunger that Satan tempted Him, therefore His fast was apparently from food.

Fasting Under the New Covenant

Some translations do not include the word "fasting" in reference to Jesus' statement in Matthew 17:21 and Mark 9:29 where He was explaining why the disciples were unable to cast out an evil spirit because of unbelief. He said, "This kind can come forth by nothing, but prayer and fasting." However, this statement does not teach a merit-based fast; rather, Jesus is speaking of a prayer-life or a fasted-life. The reason for that, of course, is because faith rises in the heart of one who is given to the Word of God through prayer and fasting. Times of prayer and fasting close down the sense-gates to your life and enhances a focus on God's Word. It is from hearing His Word that faith comes.

Under the New Covenant, fasting was not associated with repentance or humbling oneself, but rather in seeking God and ministering to Him. The church leaders in Antioch were in prayer and fasting and ministering to the Lord when the first apostolic call came for Paul and Barnabas to go forth as apostles (Acts 13:1-3). It seems that fasting was a normal part of their worship and seeking God's direction.

Fasting was also associated with church order and the ordaining of leaders. When Paul and Barnabas were being sent out, the leaders once again entered into fasting and prayer in order to lay hands on them for the apostolic sending. After going forth in this apostolic ministry, Paul and Barnabas ordained elders as church leaders and committed them to the Lord through the same process of prayer, fasting, and laying on of hands.

How Shall I Fast?

Unless one has had experience in fasting and knows that God has called them to an extended fast, a fast for more than three to seven days is not recommended. I suggest that you start with a meal. Take your lunch break and get alone for prayer and meditation. After experiencing that discipline, extend your fasting to a full day with eating the evening meal with your family. Then try a twenty-four-hour period. Once you have done that, then consider a three to five day fast.

When you fast, remember your purpose for the fast. It may be to seek God for spiritual strength, to have Him help you with your desires and habits, or to find direction from the Holy Spirit. Your heart should also include others when you fast according to Isaiah 58. And above all, your fasting should be to minister unto the Lord.

Fasting is a spiritual discipline and will be more successful with times of prayer and a prayerful attitude. Prepare yourself for extra time meditating the Scriptures. You may find a renewed awareness and sensitivity to the Holy Spirit during a fast. Spiritual awareness seems to greatly increase during and after a fast.

Not much physical preparation is needed for a short fast, except maybe the elimination of caffeine and sugar intakes to guard against headaches. Some people want to gorge themselves before a fast, thinking it will help. The opposite is true. A healthy meal of fruit and vegetables will be to your benefit before starting even a three-day fast.

It is better to have a fasted lifestyle than to go on a fast for long periods of time. The Bible records Jesus fasting at the beginning of His ministry with the forty-day fast; however, with the disciplined life of Jesus, it is easy to understand that He lived a fasted life. His life was a life of prayer and dedication to the Father, which no doubt included regular short times of fasting to be alone in prayer.

When Jesus said not to announce your fast, He did not intend for you to deny that you are fasting in order to cover it up. His intent is for us not make it public or draw attention to the fact. If you are invited to dinner with a Christian friend, simply go and let them know that you enjoy their fellowship, but you will not be eating since you are fasting. If an unbeliever invites you to eat, it might be best to interrupt your fast for a period. Remember, fasting is unto the Lord, so that He will lead you.

Application

1. What are the three Christian disciplines in which Jesus' expected His followers to participate?

   1) _____

   2) _____

   3) _____

2. Define fasting.

   _____

   _____

   _____

3. Explain the different types of fasting.

   1) Absolute Fast _____

   _____

   2) Normal Fast _____

   _____

   3) Partial Fast _____

   _____

4. What statement made by Jesus is the strongest support for Christians fasting today?

   _____

   _____

   _____

5. Under the New Covenant fasting was not associated with _____ and
   _____ _____, but rather in seeking God and ministering to Him.

6. Remember to be working on this week's memory verses. Go to the appendix and meditate upon the verses for this week.

Discipline of Giving

Giving is of the nature of God. God is love and love gives. We read in the Gospel of John, "God so loved the world that He gave . . ." (John 3:16). When we love God and others, we want to give. Giving is not only a spiritual discipline, but like prayer and fasting, it honors God and is considered worship. The Bible speaks of three areas of giving. There is almsgiving, offerings, and tithes.

Almsgiving

Almsgiving is contributing to the deserving poor; those who cannot provide for themselves. Jesus said to do this without drawing attention to ourselves. To announce giving to those in need robs you of your reward. Almsgiving is to be done behind the scenes, not letting "your left hand know what your right hand is doing" (Matt 6:3). It gives dignity to those receiving the help. To announce it only embarrasses the poor and gives honor to yourself.

The early Church practiced giving to the poor. When Paul, the apostle, went up to Jerusalem to submit the gospel to the apostles that he had received from Christ, they asked nothing of him except to remember the poor. He wrote that he was very eager to do that all along (Galatians 2:10). When you give to the poor, you lend to the Lord, and the Lord will reward (Proverbs 19:17).

Freewill Offerings

Freewill offerings are when we give as we purpose in our heart. Being generous to needs and causes in the kingdom reminds us of partnering with others for ministry. The early Church gave to other Christians suffering persecution or in need. Through great generosity, no one went without. Freewill gifts were provided voluntarily, and no requirement was placed on them (Acts 5:4). Paul instructed the Christians in Corinth to set their contribution aside and give as they purposed (2 Corinthians 8, 9). This giving is of God's grace. Paul called it the "grace of giving." It honors God. Paul said, "This service that you perform is not only supplying the needs of the Lord's people but is also overflowing in many expressions of thanks to God" (2 Corinthians 9:12).

Tithing

Tithing is giving a tenth of our increase to God as a means of honoring and worshiping Him as our provider. We worship God with our tithe as they did in the Old Testament, but without ceremonial sacrifices. Christ became our sacrifice as He fulfilled any requirements for righteousness. Our sacrifice is the fruit of our lips and the offering of our bodies and possessions to His service. The tithe is an expression of our faith and submission to God's church on the earth. It is a recognition of His ownership of our lives and possessions. Tithing is an act of worship. It brings no righteousness, but it does acknowledge our faith and worship toward him as all obedience to Christ does.

When a person tithes they are turning their life into worship because tithing is taking ten percent of your increase and setting it aside for Him on a systematic basis. It automatically brings daily life to worship. When a person works hard and receives an exchange of money for their labor, they are acknowledging God as the provider and owner of their life. Tithing off the top requires honor and trust to God (Proverbs 3:9). Abraham understood that when he tithed to Melchizedek. He knew that only God could make him rich and tithing was a step of faith to declare that to be so (Genesis 14:23).

Trusting Christ's Body

Tithing requires trust in the body of Christ. It acknowledges that God provides an ordained receipt of the tithe through the local church. The church is in every locale where believers live out life in submission to one another and Christ's government through local leaders, called elders of the church.

The fact that Abraham tithed before the law demonstrates that God established the tithe and *provided a recipient of His tithe* before the ceremonial requirements of the law were established (Gen. 14:20). It was an act of worship and faith when Abraham offered his tithe to Melchizedek. When a person tithes, he is saying, "God is my source."

The tithe belongs to God. "Will a man rob God? Yet you have robbed Me! But you say, 'In what way have we robbed You?' In tithes and offerings" (Mal. 3:8). You cannot rob someone of something that is not theirs. Leviticus tells us, "And all the tithe of the land, whether of the seed of the land or of the fruit of the tree, is the LORD'S. It is holy to the LORD" (Lev. 27:30). The tithe is the Lord's. We rob God when we refuse to give back to Him what He already owns. All our life belongs to him.

In explaining the priesthood of Christ, the writer of Hebrews points out the importance of Melchizedek. He shows "how great this man was" (Hebrews. 7:4), to whom Abraham gave a tithe or tenth. Jesus is of the order of priesthood of Melchizedek. In Hebrews, we see that Jesus was present figuratively as the recipient of the tithe of Abraham. Today, all those of faith are sons of Abraham and pay tithe to Christ in the priesthood of Melchizedek. Under the New Testament, the same validity remains as He receives the tithe in the Church under the same priesthood. We can use this same argument to show that the ordained recipient of the tithe not only validates tithing but also points to the authority structure of Christ in His church. When you tithe you tithe to Christ through His Church.

Even though the word tithe is not used in the New Testament, references requiring the financing of ministry are paralleled with the requirements of the tithe in the Old Testament. We have no reason to believe the tithe has been altered, changed, or annulled. Instead, we have a greater ability, through the Spirit of grace, to meet kingdom needs. If we are under command to supply specific needs in the

New Testament, then we must believe God has given us a guide to supply those needs. That guide is the biblical tithe.

Where the priests in the Old Covenant were guardians of the temple, in the New Covenant the elders of the church have the responsibility to guard God's temple, the flock. Paul warns the elders to guard themselves and the flocks to which the Holy Spirit has made them overseers. Paul tells Timothy, elders who rule well and labor in the doctrine are to be rewarded well with financial support (1 Tim. 5:17). When writing to the Corinthians, Paul makes the leap from the Old Testament (Lev 6:16, 26; 7:6, 31), to the New Testament for us when he writes, "Do you not know that those who minister the holy things eat of the things of the temple, and those who serve at the alter partake of the offerings of the altar?" (1 Corinthians 9:13). We are not left to question this instruction in that he quotes the Lord's commandment, "that those who preach the gospel should live from the gospel" (1 Corinthians 9:14; Galatians. 6:6).

In addition to the responsibility to provide for those who labor in the word, Paul puts a requirement upon the local church to provide for those he calls *widows indeed* (1 Tim. 5:3-5, 9, 16). James tells us that true religion is to visit the fatherless and widow when they are in need. The word "visit" means to go see, look out for, and relieve. The tithe then is a means to help the widow and orphan under the New Covenant.

The stranger in the Old Testament were those who were outside of Israel and were not in the covenant. In the same manner, in the New Testament, those who are without a covenant in Christ (unbelievers) are considered strangers. We are given the great commission and a responsibility to help finance the work of evangelism and bring those into covenant with Christ. Paul expected the church to finance evangelism and ministries of the church. Where do those funds come from except the tithe? There is no reason to assume that the tithe was not used for these purposes since we have no authority to say the tithe was repealed. The New Testament tithes paid the expected support of *elders*, paid for the necessary cost of the *widows*, helped the *fatherless*, and supported *evangelism* and provided a means of *worship*.

Application

1. What are the three areas of giving? _____, _____, _____

2. What is almsgiving?

_____

_____

_____

3. In 2 Corinthians 8, Paul describes giving as a _____.

4. Write in your own words how giving becomes worship to the believer.

_____

_____

_____

5. Why does it take trust in Christ's body to worship with the tithe?

_____

_____

_____

6. Since Christ is of the order of Melchizedek, when we tithe to whom are we giving?

_____

7. Name the five areas the tithe helps to support.

_____

_____

_____

_____

Overcoming with the Holy Spirit

In our past lessons, we have addressed the Father's love, His call upon our lives, and the redemptive work of Christ. This week we discuss the Holy Spirit and His work with you. It is through His power that we can be overcomers. Paul, tells us the Holy Spirit can do more than we can imagine. He wrote, "Now to him who is able to do immeasurably more than all we ask or imagine, according to His power that is at work within us" (Ephesians 3:20).

You have the best deal imaginable. Not only is His power at work in you to do what is right, but it is God who places the desire in you in the first place. That is a winning situation. While encouraging the Christians in Philippi, Paul wrote, "For it is God who works in you to will and to act according to His good purpose" (Philippians 2:13).

The Deity of The Holy Spirit

The Holy Spirit is God as the third member of the Godhead. The doctrine of the Triune God is taught throughout the Old and New Testament. It is called the doctrine of the Trinity (God the Father, Son, and Holy Spirit). It is addressed in the "Apostles' Creed." It is named the Apostles' Creed not because the apostles wrote it but because it contains a summary of their teachings. It sets forth their doctrine in simplicity, brevity, and order.

> *I believe in God, the Father almighty, creator of heaven and earth. I believe in Jesus Christ, God's only Son, our Lord, who was conceived by the Holy Spirit, born of the Virgin Mary, suffered under Pontius Pilate, was crucified, died, and was buried; He descended to hell. On the third day, He rose again; He ascended into heaven, He is seated at the right hand of the Father, and He will come again to judge the living and the dead. I believe in the Holy Spirit, the holy catholic church,[38] the communion of saints, the forgiveness of sins, the resurrection of the body, and the life everlasting. Amen*

Jesus quoted Deuteronomy 6:4, when answering one of the scribes, "Hear O Israel the Lord our God, the Lord is one" (Mark 12:29). There is one God in three persons. He is God the Father, God the Son, and God the Holy Spirit: three persons, but only one God. He is one in essence, three in person. He is both one and three at the same time.

---

38 The word "catholic" here does not refer to the Roman Catholic Church, but to the universal Church of Jesus Christ throughout the ages.

We are given a picture of the Triune God at Jesus' baptism. The Father spoke from heaven, and the Holy Spirit came upon Jesus in the form of a dove.

> *As soon as Jesus was baptized, He went up out of the water. At that moment heaven was opened, and He saw the Spirit of God descending like a dove and lighting on Him. And a voice from heaven said, "This is my Son, whom I love; with Him I am well pleased." (Matthew 3:16, 17)*

The Names of The Holy Spirit

Names given to the Holy Spirit reveal the attributes of God. There are names that relate Him to the Father. He is called: the Spirit of God (Genesis 1:2), the Spirit of your Father (Matt 10:20), the Spirit of the Lord (Luke 4:18), the Spirit of our God (1 Corinthians 6:11), the Spirit of the Living God (2 Corinthians 3:3), My Spirit (Genesis 6:3), and the Spirit of Him that raised up Jesus from the dead (Romans 8:11).

He is also related to the Son with similar names. He is called: the Spirit of Christ (Romans 8:9), the Spirit of Jesus Christ (Philippians 1:19), the Spirit of His Son (Gal 4:6), and the Spirit of the Lord as related to Jesus (Acts 5:9).[39]

The title *Holy Spirit* describes Him according to His attributes. He is called: the Spirit of holiness (Romans 1:4), the Spirit of life (Romans 8:2), Spirit of truth (John 14:17), the Spirit of grace (Hebrews 10:29), the Spirit of adoption (Romans 8:15), and the Comforter (John 14:16). He is called the Holy Spirit for more reasons than because He is holy. His work is to make us holy. Martyn Lloyd Jones explains,

> *Why, then, is He called holy? Surely, the explanation is that it is His special work to produce holiness and order in all that He does in the application of Christ's work of salvation. His objective is to produce holiness, and He does that in nature and creation, as well as in human beings. But His ultimate work is to make us a holy people, holy as the children of God.[40]*

Paul speaks of the fruit of the Spirit. The Holy Spirit bears forth fruit—the very nature, and character of God—in a Christian. The fruit of the Spirit reflects God's work in a maturing Christian. Paul identified nine fruit of the Spirit, "But the fruit of the Spirit is love, joy, peace, patience, kindness, goodness, faithfulness, gentleness, and self-control. Against such things, there is no law" (Galatians 5:22, 23). Notice the word fruit is singular and not plural. It speaks of the nine-fold characteristics of His holiness produced in the Christian. That is why it is referred to as the "fruit of the Holy Spirit."

Jesus said when the Holy Spirit comes; He will guide you into all truth. The Holy Spirit is a teacher and guide (John 16:13). The Holy Spirit will speak to you and bear testimony of Christ (John 15:26). His work includes illuminating the Scriptures to your understanding and leading you in your Christian walk. When Jesus ascended into heaven, the promise of the Father, which was the Holy Spirit, was sent

---

39 Acts 5:9—The Spirit of the Lord here in Acts is related to Christ where in Luke 4:18 it is related to the Father.
40 Martyn Lloyd Jones, *God the Holy Spirit, Great Doctrines of the Bible* (Wheaton, IL: Crossway Books, 1997), 8.

to earth to abide in all believers. Since the Day of Pentecost in Acts 2, the Holy Spirit has been at work baptizing new believers into the Body of Christ, which is His Church.

Beginning on the Day of Pentecost, the Holy Spirit came to dwell in all believers; however, that does not mean He was not present before. He was present at creation (Genesis 1:2), He worked through the prophets and leaders in the Old Testament (Numbers 11:25; 27:18; Isaiah 63:11), filled John the Baptist from birth (Luke 1:15), and filled his mother Elizabeth and His father Zechariah (Luke 1:41, 67). As God, the Holy Spirit was active in empowering certain leaders and individuals for great exploits, but it was on the Day of Pentecost that He was made to dwell in all who believe.

The Holy Spirit not only dwells in believers, but He is present in the earth to keep order and to sustain creation (Psalm 104:30). He is at work to give common blessings to all mankind and to provide for the just and the unjust (Matt 5:45). This is called God's common grace.

Application

1. Write out Philippians 2:13 in your own words.

_____

_____

2. Explain how the Trinity is pictured in the baptism of Jesus (Matthew 3:16, 17).

_____

_____

3. Give the names of the Holy Spirit that relate to:

The Father 1) _____

2) _____

3) _____

4) _____

5) _____

The Son   1) _____

2) _____

3) _____

4) _____

4. Give three of the six names given to the Holy Spirit that describe His attributes. Give a verse for each name.

1) _____

2) _____

3) _____

5. Why is He called holy?

_____

_____

_____

The Person of The Holy Spirit

The Holy Spirit is a person. He is not merely a force or power. We must take great care to see the Holy Spirit as a person and not just an influence. One reason some people may find it hard to understand the Holy Spirit as a person is because He is described throughout the Scriptures by symbols such as fire, wind, water, oil,[41] and a dove. For example, John said that Jesus would baptize with the Holy Spirit and fire (Luke 3:16). At Jesus' baptism, the Holy Spirit came upon Him in the form of a dove (Matthew 3:16). And once, when Jesus spoke of the Holy Spirit, He said it would be like streams of living water flowing out of believers (John 7:38). On the Day of Pentecost, the Holy Spirit was poured out, and there was a sound of a mighty rushing wind as tongues of fire separated and sat upon each person present (Acts 2:2).

People may have difficulty in understanding how the Holy Spirit is a person because He does not have a body. Ralph Riggs addresses this in his book, *The Spirit Himself*. He writes, "The Holy Spirit is a spirit, like God the Father, and so the Holy Spirit is also a person. His omnipresence is an impossible conception if we confine Him to a body. Having the faculties and attributes of a person constitutes a person, whether or not that person customarily resides in a body."[42]

The Holy Spirit is as personal as a person. The early church experienced a relationship with the Holy Spirit in the decision when gathered in Jerusalem for the first council. As they concluded how to deal with a division between Jewish believers and Gentile Christians, the Scripture records the words, "It seemed good to the Holy Spirit and to us" (Acts 15:28). He was personally involved in their decision, and He was named as part of the agreement.

He Can Be Sinned Against

Sins against the Holy Spirit reveal that He is a person and that He is God. The Bible mentions at least six sins that can be against the Holy Spirit.

1. Grieving the Holy Spirit (Ephesians 4:30)—To grieve the Holy Spirit means to cause sorrow by refusing to put off the old man and walk after the fruit of the Spirit. He grieves because of His love for us and dwells in us.

2. Resisting the Holy Spirit (Acts 7:51)—To resist the Holy Spirit means to oppose, withstand, or strive against Him. People resist the Holy Spirit when they think they have their lives in control and they

---

41 Oil was used for anointing Exodus 30:25,30; 1 Samuel 16:13; 1 Kings 19:16
42 Ralph M. Riggs, *The Spirit Himself* (Springfield, MO: Gospel Publishing House 1968), 4.

can come to God on their terms. The writer of Hebrews warned against testing God and turning from Him with rebellious and hardened hearts of unbelief (Hebrews 3:12).

3. Quenching the Holy Spirit (1 Thessalonians 5:19)—To quench the Holy Spirit means to extinguish the blaze of desire and operation of the Spirit.

4. Lying to the Holy Spirit (Acts 5:3)—To lie to the Holy Spirit is to intentionally deceive by giving misleading or false information and by acting in a way to represent untruth.

5. Insulting the Holy Spirit (Hebrews 10:29)—To insult the Holy Spirit is to cause a reproach to Him. God was displeased with Israel "when they often rebelled against Him in the desert" (Psalm 78:40, 41).

6. Blaspheming the Holy Spirit (Matthew 12:22-32)—To blaspheme the Holy Spirit means to willfully and maliciously reject and slander the Holy Spirit's work attesting to Christ, and claim it as the work of Satan. This is not simply unbelief or rejection of the truth, but it is to slander by attributing out of hatred the very work of God, the Holy Spirit, to the influence of Satan. It is the evil work of Satan to deceive and attribute God's glorious works to Satan himself.

If someone should ask if he has committed this unpardonable sin, he has not. The simple evidence of that person being concerned about God's grace and mercy upon him, proves he has not blasphemed the Holy Spirit. Such a person would never ask the question. There would be no concern of blaspheming.

He Is Personally Involved in Your Salvation

He Draws (John 6:44; Ephesians 4:4)—The free offer of salvation is given by the calling of the Holy Spirit through grace (Rom 8:30).

He Convicts (John 16:8)—It is the Holy Spirit who takes the initiative and convicts a sinner, revealing to him his sin and need of God.

He Regenerates (John 3:5; Titus 3: 5)—The work of the Holy Spirit in salvation is to bring the sinner to life through His creative quickening power.

He Converts (2 Thessalonians 2:13)—We are saved through the sanctifying work of the Holy Spirit through belief in the truth.

He Justifies (1 Corinthians 6:11)—The sinner is declared "just" or righteous in the name of Jesus Christ and by the Holy Spirit.

He Adopts (Romans 8:15)—The believer is admitted into the rights and privileges of sonship by the power of the Holy Spirit.

He Sanctifies (Galatians 5:22, 23)—We are made holy by His fruit in our lives. It is the work of the Holy Spirit to bring forth sanctification.

He Abides (John 14:17; 1 Corinthians 3:16)—All believers have the abiding presence of the Holy Spirit. We are the temple of the Holy Spirit.

He Seals (2 Corinthians 2:22)—The Holy Spirit seals the believer as a deposit of what is to come until the redemption of those who are God's possession.

His Gifts Are Active Today

While some Christians are taught that the gifts of the Spirit ended with the first-century apostles, the gifts of the Spirit are flowing and operating through millions of Christians around the world. Those who reject the abiding validity of the gifts today reason from 1 Corinthians 13, where it says,

> *Love never fails. But whether there are prophecies, they will fail; whether there are tongues, they will cease; whether there is knowledge, it will vanish away. For we know in part and we prophesy in part. But when that which is perfect has come, then that which is in part will be done away.* (1 Corinthians 13:8-10)

They claim that "perfect" refers to the canonization of the Bible. Even though the Bible is perfect, there is nothing in the context of the Scriptures to make us believe the perfect is referring to the canonization of the Scriptures. However, the word "perfect," suggest the completeness and maturity of the Church at the resurrection. It is explained well in *Matthew Henry Commentary*,

> *He takes occasion hence to show how much better it will be with the Church hereafter than it can be here. A state of perfection is in view (v. 10): When that which is perfect shall come, then that which is in part shall be done away. When the end is once attained, the means will, of course, be abolished.*[43]

All the gifts of Christ and the Holy Spirit continue to operate in Christ's body until the resurrection of the dead and the end of all things. Then, and only at that time, can we say the perfect has come, when Christ Himself appears at the end of history.

---

43 Matthew Henry Commentary—1 Corinthians 13:8-13 PP2, III

Application

1. Power is one of the Holy Spirit's characteristics, but we must take great care to see the Holy Spirit as a _____ and not just an _____.

2. There are at least four symbols of the Holy Spirit. List them and give an example.

   1) _____

   2) _____

   3) _____

   4) _____

3. Fill in the blanks with the type of sin against the Holy Spirit that is described in each of the following.

   _____—It is because the Holy Spirit loves that this sin is possible.

   _____—This sin is an attempt to put out the fire of the Holy Spirit.

   _____—This sin brought death in Acts 5.

   _____—The sin that is unforgiven.

   _____—Stephen said the Jews committed this sin by being stiff-necked.

   _____—This sin brings a reproach to Him.

4. The lesson identifies nine aspects of the Holy Spirit's work in salvation. What are they?

   1) _____

   2) _____

   3) _____

   4) _____

   5) _____

   6) _____

   7) _____

   8) _____

   9) _____

Baptism with The Spirit

When you became a Christian, you received the Holy Spirit to abide in you. No man can say Jesus is Lord except by the Holy Spirit (1 Corinthians 12:3). A Christian is someone who has been born of the Spirit, and in whom the Holy Spirit has done the work of regeneration. If someone does not have the Holy Spirit, he does not belong to Christ (Romans 8:9). So, by definition, a Christian is someone who has the Holy Spirit living in him. However, a person may be a believer in the abiding Holy Spirit and not experience the fullness of the Holy Spirit operating in their life.

When you come to Jesus in salvation, the Holy Spirit baptizes you into the body of Christ. This is an internal spiritual baptism that takes place in the life of the believer (1 Corinthians 12:13; Romans 6:4). As a result of this inward baptism, we are instructed to follow the Lord's example in an outward testimony of that work through water baptism. Jesus gave us this example in being baptized in water Himself by John the Baptist (Matthew 3:13-17). What then is the baptism of the Spirit? What did Jesus mean when He told His disciples to wait in Jerusalem until they had been baptized with the Holy Spirit? Jesus gave this command before He ascended into heaven, "Do not leave Jerusalem, but wait for the gift my Father promised, which you have heard me speak about. For John baptized with water, but in a few days you will be baptized with the Holy Spirit" (Acts 1:4, 5).

The disciples had experienced a regeneration of the Spirit before Pentecost when Jesus breathed on them to receive the Holy Spirit (John 20:22). There is no doubt that when Jesus breathed on them, they received the Holy Spirit even though this was before the Day of Pentecost. They did receive the Spirit, but they were not baptized with the Holy Spirit. That is why Jesus told them to not depart from Jerusalem until they had received the promise of the Father.

Another example of people becoming believers first without the baptism of the Spirit is in Acts 8. When Philip went to Samaria and preached the Gospel, the Bible tells us many Samaritans believed and were baptized in water. There was great joy in the city, which is evidence of the Holy Spirit's presence in them. When the apostles heard about those who received the Word, they sent Peter and John to pray for them to receive the Holy Spirit. This account demonstrates believers who have received Christ and conversion, yet another experience came to them when they were prayed for by the apostles.

In Acts 9, Paul himself was converted on the road to Damascus, received Christ, called Him Lord, and was praying to the Lord before he received the fulness of the Spirit. The man named Ananias was sent to lay hands on Him to be healed and receive the Holy Spirit. Ananias did not preach to him to be saved because Paul had already met Christ; however, it was not until hands were laid on Paul that he received the Holy Spirit. Why do we see these accounts of people receiving Christ as Lord and yet having hands laid on them for the Holy Spirit to come on them? Were they without the Holy Spirit in their conversion? Obviously not, but these are examples of believers receiving the fullness of the Holy Spirit.

Once again in Acts 19, we find another example of converts being baptized in water and then hands were laid on them to receive the Holy Spirit. Paul was traveling along the upper coast and came to Ephesus. He found a group of twelve people who were disciples of John. The first question Paul asked them was, "Did you receive the Holy Spirit when you believed?" This sounds like you can be a believer without the Holy Spirit. However, Paul knew well that no one could be a believer apart from the Holy Spirit. Why would he have asked that question? At that time, he assumed they were fully taught in Christ's baptism. It wasn't until after that question that he discovered they were only baptized unto John. Therefore, by Paul's question, it is clear that he is speaking of a fuller experience of the Spirit. That fact is confirmed when he lays hands on them, they receive the Holy Spirit, and it was evidenced by speaking in tongues and prophesying.

Now, it is possible for someone to be baptized with the Holy Spirit virtually concurrent with receiving Christ at salvation. This happened in Acts 10 at Cornelius' house. While Peter was speaking to them about salvation and the kingdom, the Holy Spirit fell on them, and it occurred simultaneously as they believed. It happened to those Gentiles just like it did the Jews on the Day of Pentecost, for they spoke in tongues and magnified God.

Evidence of The Baptism

Many people have given testimony of an experience of new power for ministry, and vitality to live the Christian life, from receiving this baptism. They have spoken of an increased hunger for prayer, power for witnessing, and the receiving and manifestation of spiritual gifts. Scripture gives several accounts of phenomenal occurrences taking place in the lives of believers who have been filled with the Spirit. All of these point to the power of the Holy Spirit to do the works of Jesus through the life of a believer.

On the Day of Pentecost, this experience was evidenced by people from many nations hearing Christians speak in the tongues of the non-believers' native lands. The joy and power were so evident that observers marveled while others doubted. Some thought by their behavior that they must be drunk (Acts 2:1-13).

In Acts 8 when the Samaritans received the Holy Spirit, it does not say they spoke in tongues, but something phenomenal must have taken place. We know this because Simon, the sorcerer, wanted to buy the ability to lay hands on people and have them receive the Holy Spirit. If nothing outwardly occurred, such as tongues or prophecy, then he would not have bargained for that opportunity. What did he see that he wanted to be able to bestow?

When the Gentiles in Acts 10 received the Holy Spirit at Cornelius' house, they spoke in tongues and magnified God. The disciples in Acts 19 at Ephesus spoke in tongues, as well, and prophesied when they received. In the accounts of the New Testament of people being baptized or filled with the Holy

Spirit, the most common occurrence was speaking in tongues. There were other manifestations as well, such as healings, great joy, prophesying, and boldness.

A word of caution: we must take great care in not dividing Christians into two classes, those who are spirit-filled and those who are ordinary. All believers have the same Holy Spirit even though they may not have experienced the full expression.

What Is Speaking in Tongues?

When a believer speaks to God in a language they have never learned on their own; it is called speaking in tongues (1 Corinthians 14:2). According to 1 Corinthians 13:1, this might be a language spoken somewhere else in the world or by angels. When one prays in tongues, he is speaking divine mysteries from his spirit to God. Tongues spoken in a public meeting is called a "manifestation" or "gift" of the Spirit. In that instance, it is to be interpreted, so others are encouraged (1 Corinthians 14:24, 25). When interpreted speaking in tongues is equal to prophecy. However, in private, Paul said he prayed in the spirit more than all those in the Corinthian church (1 Corinthians 14:18). He also indicated that he chose to pray or sing in the spirit when he wrote, "What shall I do? I will pray with my spirit, but I will also pray with my understanding; I will sing with my spirit, but I will also sing with my understanding" (1 Corinthians 14:15).

To pray in the spirit includes tongues. That is what Paul means when he says he will pray with his spirit. Here in this chapter, Paul is dealing with the gift of tongues or the manifestation of the Holy Spirit in public worship. The gift of tongues is to be interpreted and is for a different purpose than when praying in private. When Paul said, he prayed in tongues more than the entire church he was not talking about public worship but private prayer. We know that because he said he would rather speak five words with understanding in public than ten thousand words in tongues. When praying in private, it requires no interpretation and it not limited. This prayer language is available for all those who have received this baptism or full experience. It is for the encouragement and strengthening of the individual believer as he prays divine mysteries to God (1 Corinthians 14:4; Jude 20). Seek earnestly all that God has for you.

Application

1. By definition a Christian is someone who has the _____ _____ living in him.

2. Give and explain at least one biblical example of people who were filled or baptized with the Holy Spirit after conversion.

    _____

    _____

    _____

    _____

3. While it is important to recognize evidence in the life of the believer who has received the fullness or the baptism of the Spirit, it is very important that we take great care in guarding against causing division. Explain.

    _____

    _____

    _____

    _____

4. In the accounts of the New Testament of people being baptized or being filled with the Holy Spirit, the most common occurrence was _____.

5. Explain the two purposes of speaking in tongues and give proof text.

    1) When in a public church meeting.

    _____

    _____

    2) When in private prayer.

    _____

    _____

Gifts of The Spirit

Gifts of the Spirit are just that; they function as the Holy Spirit wills in the life of the believer. The Greek word for "gift" is "grace, kindness, or graciousness." God graciously desires to reveal Himself through the life of the believer. Every good and perfect gift comes down from above and is from the Father (James 1:17). So, any grace or operation of the Holy Spirit is considered a gift. Jesus said, "Signs will accompany those who believe" (Mark 16:17a). Those signs are by the power of the Holy Spirit.

Manifestations of The Spirit

The Holy Spirit manifests Himself in nine different ways. These nine manifestations are also called gifts of the Spirit. They are listed in 1 Corinthians 12:7-10. The Greek word translated as manifestation means to exhibit, reveal or shine forth. When the Holy Spirit wills, He may manifest Himself in one or more of these nine ways to reveal the work of Christ.

An easy way to remember these manifestations is to place them in categories that relate to their purpose. The Bible does not categorize these gifts, but we do so only for simplicity of understanding. We list these as revelation, power, and utterance.

Gifts of Revelation

Revelatory gifts refer to the Holy Spirit revealing His mind and knowledge to and through believers. These gifts may come by a vision, dream, prophecy, tongues, and interpretation, or by the speaking of the Holy Spirit in the heart of a believer.

Word of Wisdom (Acts 27:10, 11, 22, 23)—A manifestation of the Holy Spirit that allows a person to receive the mind of God on what and how something is to take place. The term "word" comes from the Greek *logos* meaning the matter of the subject or message. Wisdom means the ability to use knowledge to know what to do. Therefore, we can say that a word of wisdom deals with a revealed portion, or part of the plans and purposes of God. It is only a "word," therefore it is but a portion of God's wisdom. That portion is revealed by the Holy Spirit as He wills.

Word of Knowledge (Acts 5:1-9)—A manifestation of the Holy Spirit that gives a fragment of divine knowledge that is presently taking place or has happened. This gift is a portion or part of supernatural facts and information that a person would not normally know. It deals with the past and present, while the word of wisdom addresses the future. A person operating in a word of knowledge would know by the Holy Spirit something that God wanted to reveal about what has taken place or is presently happening.

Discerning of Spirits (Acts 16:16-18)—The ability of God to distinguish by what spirit an action or manifestation is occurring. Discerning of spirits may deal with angelic host or demons. It is often erroneously called the "gift of discernment," but it is the gift of "discerning of spirits." We are told to test the spirits (1 John 4:1); however, this manifestation is more than that. It is when the Holy Spirit allows you to discern by spiritual knowledge that a word is being spoken or action is being taken that is caused or motivated by a spirit. This includes a spiritual vision of a spirit or angel as God allows.

Gifts of Power

Gifts of power refer to the working of God's might in believers to do the works of Jesus here on earth. We can put gifts of healings, working of miracles, and special faith in this category.

Gifts of Healings (Acts 3:7; 5:15,16)—The manifestation of God's power to heal sickness. This gift is listed in the plural. This is best demonstrated in Christ's life when He healed so many different kinds of illnesses and infirmities. It is reasonable to believe that God has gifts of healings for various means of ministry to those who are afflicted with different illnesses. The operation of this gift is different than a progressive healing that can occur through prayer and faith. Gifts of healings is an immediate manifestation of the cure or corrected ailment.

Working of Miracles (Acts 13:11; 20:10)—The manifestation of God's power to alter natural laws and operations. This gift is the intervention of the normal course of nature. Jesus did many miracles and even began His ministry by the miracle of turning water into wine. When He fed the five thousand with five loaves of bread and two fish, and when He walked on water, He was causing the course of natural things to be changed. Healing and miracles can work together when a person is raised from the dead, or a lame person is healed. Miracles and gifts of healings are listed fourth and fifth in the order of gifts appointed by God in the church which reveals the importance of these gifts. Paul wrote, "And God has appointed these in the church: first apostles, second prophets, third teachers, after that miracles, then gifts of healings . . ." (1 Corinthians 12:28).

Gift of Faith (Acts 3:1-10)—Special faith received at the moment or duration for a particular need. All faith is from God, but this faith is called "special faith"[44] and is listed as a manifestation of the Holy Spirit. A believer's faith grows, but this gift of faith comes at special times as the Holy Spirit wills. Thus, it is a manifestation of the Holy Spirit. There is a boldness with this gift that goes beyond the faith individuals might normally have. It often comes when regular faith ends and miracles are needed. It may operate along with several other gifts. A gift of faith remains stedfast even when something is far off in the future.

---

44 The *Amplified Bible* and the Weymouth translation uses this term.

Gifts of Utterance

This category is listed as such because each of these gifts come through speaking. They bring encouragement, exhortation, and strength to others. Prophecy is for the edification of others. Tongues spoken in public require interpretation and equals prophecy in value when interpreted.

Gift of Prophecy (Acts 21:10)—A word spoken by the inspiration of the Holy Spirit to bring an understanding of the will and purposes of God. This gift is the most explained, most promoted, and most mentioned. A good portion of 1 Corinthians 14 is devoted to prophecy. Paul tells us that prophecy is to be judged and limited when in public meeting (1 Corinthians 14:29). This gift is given to build up and encourage the church. It is different from the ministry of the prophet in that not everyone who prophesies is a prophet and Paul said he desired that everyone would prophesy. When a person prophesies they do so according to their faith (Romans 12:6). It is not considered equal to the written Word; that is why it must be judged. Paul tells us we prophesy in part. Therefore, prophecy is limited (1 Corinthians 13:9b).

Gift of Tongues (1 Corinthians 14:27)—The ability to speak in a language, by the Holy Spirit, which the speaker has not learned. The gift of tongues is to be used in the public meetings only when it can be interpreted; otherwise, the individual is instructed to pray with the language that others can understand (1 Corinthians 14:13, 19). It is called speaking in different or various kinds of tongues. This gift is not just speaking in tongues but various kinds of tongues. That differentiates it from believers praying privately in tongues. Speaking in tongues is available for all believers, but the gift of tongues, here in 1 Corinthians 14, is given only as the Holy Spirit wills. This gift of speaking various tongues is to be interpreted and equals prophecy in value to the encouragement of others.

Gift of Interpretation of Tongues (1 Corinthians 14:5, 13)—The ability to interpret by giving the sense of what has been delivered with the gift of tongues. Notice, it is not a translation but rather an interpretation. It is an interpretation of what the Holy Spirit desires to express not a word for word translation.

Tongues spoken in private can be prayed at will, but the leadership of the Holy Spirit manifests the gift of tongues. That is why there must be an interpretation in the public meeting. The gift of tongues, when interpreted strengthens the congregation of believers. When an interpretation is given, like prophecy, it is by faith and by the Holy Spirit. Since it is not a translation, it is an interpreting of what the Holy Spirit is saying through tongues.

Application

1. Define the word manifestation as it is used in regard to the gifts of the Spirit.

_____

_____

_____

2. List the three revelatory gifts and describe them in your own words.

1) _____

_____

2) _____

_____

3) _____

_____

3. This gift is a manifestation of God's power to alter natural laws and operations. What gift is it?

_____

4. What is the difference between faith that a believer has from hearing the Word of God and the gift of faith?

_____

_____

5. What is the most explained, most promoted, and most mentioned gift?

_____

6. For the gift of tongues to be equal to prophecy, what must take place?

_____

_____

7. Be sure and remember to work on this week's memory verses.

Living A Spirit-Led Life

A person may believe in Christ and know they have the Holy Spirit in them, yet not understand they can have a relationship with the Holy Spirit. The Holy Spirit is our guide (John 16:13). He is our helper, teacher, and comforter (John 14:26). According to the Scriptures, He is in us, with us, and comes on us. He dwells in us from conversion and comes alongside us to help us. He also comes on us to empower us. To be a Spirit-led believer is to live a life being sensitive to the presence of the Holy Spirit in you.

He is your chief partner in everything you do. Recognizing the ever presence of the Holy Spirit in your life be the beginning of walking as a Spirit-led Christian.

What Does It Mean to Be Led?

First of all, I should point out that since you have the Spirit of adoption and you belong to God, you are being led by the Spirit in the strictest sense of the word, even if you do not realize it. That is true because you are not of the flesh but the Spirit. In keeping with the context of Romans 8, to be of the flesh is to be an unbeliever. However, to fully enjoy your Christian walk you must become developed in listening to the Lord for guidance in your life. Paul writes, "For as many as are led by the Spirit of God, these are sons of God" (Romans 8:14).

There are two extremes in our Christian walk. One is to think that if we are led by the Spirit, we have no responsibilities to plan, work, or organize our life for the purposes of God. God is just going to lead us, and we need not make plans. Some Christians who have emphasized this approach to being led by the Spirit are often criticized, and rightfully so if they become so mystical that everyday responsibilities are neglected. That is why the Word of God must be an equal balance in your life as a believer. God leads us through His Word and by His Spirit. Being led by the Spirit is always in agreement with the Scriptures. The second extreme is to think that it is left up to you, and if you don't make something happen, it won't. These Christians fall into the trap on the opposite spectrum with their confidence in their intellect, power of reason, and knowledge. These analytical Christians must guard against becoming too critical of anything that seems the least bit spiritual.

Understanding Your Spirit and Soul

God is spirit, and we have communion with Him in our spirit. God brings things to our mind, which is in your soul, but we hear from Him in our spirit. His voice may be a perception or a gentle nudging. It is important to listen to His voice within because your mind and emotions can be distracted with life. When God speaks, it is like hearing it inside your spirit and in your mind at the same time. You perceive in your spirit and think in your mind.

The Bible speaks about our spirit and soul as being different (1 Thessalonians 5:23). Your soul is made up of your mind, will, and emotion. The Scriptures say your soul considers, knows, and remembers; and this speaks of your mind.[45] Your soul also chooses, refuses, and seeks; therefore, that part is your will.[46] When you experience joy, grief, or other emotions, those come from your soul as well.[47] Consequently, we know that our soul is made up of our mind, will, and emotion.

Your spirit has three aspects as well: conscience, communion, and intuition. It is in your conscience that you know right and wrong. Paul said in Romans 9:1 that his conscience bore witness with the Holy Spirit, and Romans 8:16 his spirit did the same; thus, we see that our conscience is an aspect of our spirit.

Jesus said that true worshippers worship in spirit (John 4:24). To worship is to commune with God. Luke 1:47 says, "My spirit rejoices in God my savior." This means the human spirit has contact with God in worship. Thus, it is with your spirit that you have communion.

You perceive the things of God in your spirit as well. Paul perceived by the Spirit that a voyage he was on would end in a shipwreck (Acts 27:9, 10). At times Jesus perceived in His spirit the thoughts of men (Mark 2:8). Though Jesus was God, He was also a man and operated in the power of the Holy Spirit. When Jesus knew their thoughts, it was by a word of knowledge, which is a manifestation of the Holy Spirit. He was hearing from the Father in His spirit. That is how we hear God. Your spirit is the part in which you have communion with God or perceive the voice of God. It is possible for God to speak audibly but that is not necessary, for though we have a body, we are spiritual beings.

Trust the Holy Spirit to Speak

Many times, the Holy Spirit speaks through a nudging, impression, or urging that comes to your heart ever so gentle. At first, you may question the validity of His voice. It is appropriate to test and see if it is God. Many people hear from God, but they assume that it is only their thoughts. While there is a difference between perceiving in your spirit and thinking something in your mind, it may seem indistinguishable by a new believer. You cannot afford to accept every thought or whim that comes to you as being from God; however, through maturity and experience, you can grow to know that the Holy Spirit is leading you.

Start by listening to God during and after your prayer time. As you meditate upon Scripture, learn to listen inside your spirit. Ask God to reveal His will and insight on matters. Listen and write down what you are sensing. Talk to Christians who are more mature to see if what you hear in your spirit lines

---

45 Proverbs 2:10; 19:2; 24:14; Psalm 139:14; 13:2; Lamentations 3:20
46 Job 7:15; 6:7; 1 Chronicles 22:19
47 Isaiah 61:10; Psalm 86:4; 1 Samuel 30:6; Judges 10:16

up with Scripture and conventional Christian teaching. Test these perceptions with time and godly wisdom. You will soon learn to decipher the difference between your thoughts and those of God.

Don't expect the Holy Spirit to always speak to you the same way. It is His voice that He desires for you to hear, not the means, lest you become vulnerable to experiences and miss God. For that reason, it is best not to seek experiences, but rather seek God. While you seek Him in prayer, God will use many ways to speak to you. Remember and mark the occasion when you last knew for sure that God was speaking. Ask yourself what you felt and sensed about His voice. As you become more accustomed to hearing from Him, you will learn when He is about to speak or is speaking.

You can be assured that whether it is through one of the manifestations of the Holy Spirit or a gentle nudging in your spirit, you can hear the voice of God. Some people think they are not hearing from God because they expect certain experiences when He is leading and guiding them all along.

As you increase your prayer life, you may be led to pray with great urgency in your spirit and yet never know specifically for what or whom you are praying. It seems like God may be saying something, but you only have an urgency to pray. This is part of intercessory prayer and is the work of the Spirit in a believer. These times of prayer may include groaning and heavy sighs mixed with praying in tongues (Rom 8:26-28). Cherish these times of prayer and alter what you are doing to spend as much time as you can when this urgency to pray comes. Pray until the burden lifts. Finish praying by thanking God for the Spirit's leading.

Many Christians only see the Holy Spirit as a force or power to anoint and bless them. Though He is powerful, He is more than power. He is God and desires for us to communion with Him personally. Paul writes, "May the grace of the Lord Jesus Christ, and the love of God, and the fellowship of the Holy Spirit be with you all" (2 Corinthians 13:14). The word translated "fellowship" is from the Greek word *koinonia*, meaning communion, partnering, and sharing with intimacy.

Even though we are instructed to pray to the Father in the name of Jesus, we are encouraged to communion with the Holy Spirit. To commune is to become intimate. The more aware one is of the presence of the Holy Spirit the easier it is to be led by the Spirit. He has come alongside each believer to help and dwells in us as a guide. Learn to listen to the still small voice of the Spirit.

Application

1. Often there are two extremes when it comes to our walk as a Christian and being led by the Spirit. Explain these in your own words.

_____

_____

_____

_____

2. Name the three parts of the soul.

1) _____

2) _____

3) _____

3. Name the three aspects of the spirit.

1) _____

2) _____

3) _____

4. Many times, the Holy Spirit speaks through a _____, _____, or _____ that comes to your heart ever so gently.

5. Spend a few minutes praying over a matter. Pray in the spirit. Ask God to speak to you concerning the situation. After prayer, listen in your heart to see if you are hearing. If so, write it down. If you do not hear something right away, continue to listen throughout the day.

_____

_____

_____

_____

_____

Overcoming by Serving

The Church is the community of God that lives under the authority of Christ who is in charge of the kingdom. It is called the kingdom of our Lord and of His Christ (Revelation 11:15). The church is the agent of God on the earth to manifest His kingdom. Christ is the head of the Church. We are His body.

Up to this point, we have primarily emphasized your personal walk with Christ. Now it is important that you see the value of the other members of the Church and how you fit into this relationship. The Church is Christ's body and is the actual expression of God in the earth. When you became a Christian, you were automatically made a member of His body (1 Corinthians 12:12-18). You have full rights and privileges as a member with spiritual gifts and responsibilities.

Jesus came not to be served but to serve (Matt 20:28). Learning to have a servant's heart is of great value for growing as a disciple of Christ. Serving demonstrates Christianity in a very practical way. It flows from a heart of love.

Jesus gave us a clear example of servanthood and how we are to relate to others. What he taught about serving was contrary to the accepted cultural norm.

> Jesus said to them, "The kings of the Gentiles lord it over them; and those who exercise authority over them call themselves Benefactors. But you are not to be like that. Instead, the greatest among you should be like the youngest, and the one who rules like the one who serves." (Luke 22:25, 26)

The world's idea of someone who is great is somebody who has lots of servants working for him. But Jesus comes along and turns that idea upside down. He says the greatest is someone who is helping others and is willing to serve. In the world, leaders exercise authority over others for their benefit, but in the kingdom of God that is not to be. Our calling is to be great servants benefiting others by helping them become what God has called them to be. That is Jesus' idea of serving. That is how Paul the apostle saw himself, a slave or bondservant of Jesus Christ; and as a result, he was willing to become a servant to all (1 Corinthians 9:9).

Submitting to His Kingdom

A true test of a servant's heart is the willingness to support and submit to what belongs to someone else. This involves more than an occasional good deed; it requires a humble and submissive spirit at all times. In His teaching on money, Jesus declared that if one cannot be trusted with what belongs to another, then he will not be given his own (Luke 16:12). This is true in every area of life, particularly with authority.

As a member of Christ's body, you must learn to relate to the local church. The local church is the expression of Christ's body in every locale. It is on this ground where a true disciple's willingness to submit begins to be revealed.

To Whom Do You Submit?

Paul taught that we are to submit one to another (Ephesians. 5:21), each one esteeming the other better than themselves (Philippians 2:3), without regard to a person's social, racial, or economic state in life. We are to value one another as members of Christ. When we submit to others in Christ, we are acknowledging Christ in His Church.

Some people will say that they are submitted to Christ, but to no man. This statement reveals a distrust of God's authority in humanity. There are two ways that God primarily reveals Himself; one is by His glory, and the other is through His authority. That is why it is important to see God's authority wherever you are. Paul taught that all authority is of God and that every person must be submitted to authority. He wrote to the Christians in Rome and said,

> *Everyone must submit himself to the governing authorities, for there is no authority except that which God has established. The authorities that exist have been established by God. Consequently, he who rebels against the authority is rebelling against what God has instituted, and those who do so will bring judgment on themselves.* (Romans 13:1, 2)

God works in His Church through His authority; working through mere humanity. Watchman Nee, in his book *Spiritual Authority,* expounds on Paul's writings,

> *There is no authority except from God; all authorities have been instituted by Him. By tracing all authorities back to their source, we invariably end up with God. God is above all authorities, and all authorities are under Him. In touching God's authority, we touch God Himself. God's work is basically done not by power but by authority.*[48]

God's authority is everywhere, but spiritual authority is seen in His Church. Each member is called to submit to godly leaders that Christ has established in the local church. The writer of Hebrews declared, "Obey your leaders and submit to their authority. They keep watch over you as men who must give an account. Obey them so that their work will be a joy, not a burden, for that would be of no advantage to you" (Hebrews 13:17).

An elder, most often called a pastor in today's church culture, has been given responsibility to lead by example as they provide oversight. That responsibility includes watching over your soul and feeding you from the word of God. The writer of Hebrews tells us we make their work enjoyable when we submit and obey. It is to our benefit if we honor them through submission. Submission is for protection and guidance.

---

48 Watchman Nee, *Spiritual Authority* (New York, NY: Christian Fellowship Publishers, 1972), 22.

God considers rebellion and insubordination a severe sin. It is recorded in Numbers 16 that when Moses and Aaron were leading God's people in the wilderness, a man by the name of Korah gathered 250 supporters against them. This Korah "company" stirred up a rebellion against Moses and Aaron as leaders by accusing Moses and Aaron of taking too much authority upon themselves. They believed everyone had the same level of authority because they also heard from God. They failed to recognize what God had established as His authority. God saw their rebellion and caused the earth to open and swallow all the men and those who were with them (Numbers 16:32, 33).

It is possible to do good things, yet be out of order by acting independently of authority. We see an example of this when Aaron's sons, Nadab and Abihu, took it upon themselves to offer up incense to God without authority. They had not been told to do so, and it was considered an unauthorized fire. God brought forth His fire, consumed them, and they died (Leviticus 10:1, 2). These examples, though they seem severe, serve to show God's view of rebellion. Many churches and Christians have been hindered in their work because seeds of independence and rebellion operate in Christian workers. Though they do good work, they function in an independent state creating disunity and confusion.

We know that Satan's disposition operates in the children of disobedience, so it stands to reason that one of his strategies against believers is to deceive them into resisting God's authority. Satan knows that it hinders God's work in a person's life. That is why a disciple must learn to serve without pride and learn obedience even as Christ did. This is a powerful means of overcoming through the Church. The Church is the fullest expression of God's authority on the earth. God establishes civil and domestic authority, yet it is in His Church where the clearest representation of God's authority is seen. It takes great trust in God Himself to learn to trust His authority in mere men.

God will use authority in your life to reveal His dealings. He will often use situations to bring to the surface any traces of insubordination to His authority. It can be said; every church problem is an authority issue. It is either a misuse and abuse of authority or usurping and rebelling against authority. Understanding the principles of authority is very important. We will address that in your next lessons.

Application

1. Explain what Jesus taught about being great. He taught the opposite of the Gentile culture.

_____

_____

_____

2. A true test of a servant's heart is the willingness to _humble_ and _Submissive_ to what belongs to someone else.

3. What Bible verse tells us to submit to one another? _____

4. Who has established all authorities that exist? Give a verse of Scripture that supports your answer.

_____

_____

_____

5. What verse in the Bible tells you to submit to leaders in the church?

_____

6. How did God judge Korah and the 250 men who rebelled against God?

_____

_____

_____

7. Go to the appendix and meditate on this week's first memory verse.

Principles of Authority

The issue of authority becomes vital in the development of a disciple's maturity. Much hardship, offense, and conflict can be avoided by understanding the three principles of authority taught in today's lesson. Authority must be discerned, respected, and represented.

Authority Must Be Discerned

God has established three spheres of authority in which He has instituted His government. His authority is established in the family called domestic government (Ephesians 5:22-27; 6:1), the state called civil government (Romans 13:1-4), and the church, or ecclesiastical government (Hebrews 13:17).

Each sphere of authority stands separate and accountable to God. Civil authority has no right to overstep its boundaries into domestic authority. Civil authority cannot tell the family how to live, what to believe, how many children they are to have, or any such family function. Civil authority does have jurisdiction in matters of crimes. Church authority is also restrained from overstepping its limits into both the domestic and civil realm. The Church stands as a prophetic voice calling the civil and domestic accountable before God but does not rule those spheres. The family is subject to the Church only in matters in which the Scriptures teach. In other words, elders of the church can only confront the family in matters of transgression against God's laws. Elders have the responsibility to confront sin. However, they must appeal to the state authority for crimes. Personal preferences outside of God's word must not be imposed on the family unit by the Church authorities. The family authority can appeal up to both the church and state authority if need be. For example, family disputes can be submitted to church authority, but family crimes must be taken to civil authority. Each sphere must know its limits. Any usurping of authority from any of these three spheres only produces an unfruitful and unlawful end.

Familial Authority—The family is the very foundation of society. The individual within the family is under self-government before God and functions within the domestic authority. Adam was created by and subject to and accountable to God. When God created Eve, He gave them both responsibilities over their children. The husband is to lead his family as Christ does the church (Ephesians 5:23-31). Parents serve in the place of leadership and authority in the family.

Civil Authority—Civil authority was the second sphere instituted by God. After the fall mankind did what was right in his own eyes and evil multiplied. God brought judgment through the flood and established restraints for murder and cruelty to the creation as the first civil law (Genesis 9:5, 6). Later,

God brought forth all of His laws for ordering society. At that point, civil authority was fully established (Romans 13:4).

Church Authority—Thirdly, ecclesiastical authority was set in order by the priest and prophets of the Old Testament. God's children functioned under His government as the "church in the wilderness" (Acts 7:38). Then on the Day of Pentecost, the Holy Spirit formed the Church as the body of Christ to include all people who call upon the name of the Lord. In the Church, Christ has given five gifts, which are named in Ephesians 4:11: the apostle, prophet, evangelist, pastor, and teacher for the purpose of equipping the saints. This process is done through the work of an elder serving the local church as one of those five gifts.[49] Peter, who was an apostle and elder, charged elders to pastor and oversee the flock of God, which is the church. By doing so, they stand in a place of authority.

In the church, the authority must go beyond positional authority; it must be discerned spiritually as well. A person's authority begins with his gift and the grace of God, but it develops by serving and building relationships. It is not by gift alone. When individuals give themselves to serving others out of their gift, they gain influence. When those they serve receive their gift, a place is made for them.

Some people think they understand spiritual authority and submission, when in fact, they may be only recognizing positional authority. Positional authority is real and should be honored, but it is the lowest form of authority. As a disciple, you should practice discernment, or look for authority no matter where it is found. By recognizing authority, you are honoring God. If one sees authority only by position, then he has failed to discern God's authority in every place.

Authority Must be Respected

We are to render to authorities all that God has given them, which includes respect and honor (Romans 13:7). Submission is of the heart and attitude; therefore, this aspect of authority is vital. Even though we are not required to obey authority's demands contrary to God's laws, we must maintain an attitude of submission. When the apostles were told not to speak about Jesus, they could not obey, but they remained respectful (Acts 4:18-20). Submission is absolute, but obedience is relative to God's laws. No one has to obey a rule or law that opposes God's law.

We must be careful not to uncover authority to justify rebellion. It is too easy to point out the faults of authority only to rationalize why we have not obeyed. We are told to honor authority, not only when they deserve it or qualify in our judgment, but simply because God has placed them in our lives. Our submission should be for conscience sake and not just because of a possible correction.

Once, after being slapped in the face, Paul the apostle spoke harshly against a Jewish high priest not knowing who he was. When he was informed, he quickly recanted and gave respect even though he

---

49 2 John 1:1; 1 Peter 5:1; Acts 11:25-26; Acts 13:1; Acts 11:30

was badly mistreated (Acts 23:2-5). He corrected himself quoting Exodus 22:28, "Do not speak evil about the ruler of your people."

When King Saul was pursuing David, and David was running for his life, the opportunity was given to David to harm the king. Instead, David cut off a piece of the king's his robe while he slept just to show how close he came to defeating Saul. Nevertheless, that simple act bothered David's conscience because he knew Saul was still of God's authority, even though he was acting unrighteously.[50] David knew he must honor authority, even when the king's behavior did not merit it. You need not arbitrarily accept abuse, but how you respond to authority determines how you see God.

Authority Must Be Represented

The purpose of the authority is for protection and guidance. For authority to fulfill its purpose, it must be not only be respected but represented. To fail to represent authority is to act independently and not be in referral. When we act independently without consideration of authorities in our life, we stand without protection.

To have authority, one must be under authority (Matthew 8:5-10). Jesus is our example of being under authority and yet having authority. Jesus humbled himself and did not seek to hold on to his position with God. He was given all authority and highly exalted (Philippians 2:5-10).

For headship, there must be one willing to submit. No one in authority can demand submission. If it is demanded it is not true spiritual authority, but rather manipulation, coercion, or force. Legitimate spiritual authority functions when one who is in submission gives the right to another, through consent, to influence them. When authority is represented, submission is evident. To represent is to function in light of what the authority has desired or requested. If the subordinate has a better idea or different direction, then a referral should be made back to the authority before acting separately from the original directive. Failing to do so is to function independently.

To obey in part is the same as not obeying at all. When King Saul was instructed to destroy the enemies, he did so in part but kept some of them alive and said he wanted to offer those animals in sacrifice to God. The prophet Samuel informed him that partial obedience was not acceptable (1 Samuel 15:10-23).

---

50 1 Samuel 24

Application

1. Identify the three spheres of authority and explain each one in your own words.

    1) _____

    _____

    2) _____

    _____

    3) _____

    _____

2. Name the three principles of authority.

    1) _____

    2) _____

    3) _____

3. According to Romans 13:7, what two things are to be given to authority?

    _____

    _____

4. What is one reason why people may want to uncover authority?

    _____

5. When Paul discovered he had spoken harshly to a high priest, what scripture did he quote that shows he knew to respect authority?

    _____

    _____

6. What happens when one fails to represent authority?

    _____

    _____

Church Government

The Church is God's vehicle to establish His kingdom on the earth. His authority and government are most clearly seen in the church. In this lesson, we want to take a look at the pattern of church government according to the New Testament.

In New Testament Church government, Christ's example is the base upon which we must build. His servanthood and love are expressed through the ministry of elders and deacons for the purpose of nurturing and serving the people of God. We find a team ministry concept recognized throughout the Book of Acts and the Epistles. A team of leaders served as elders to give oversight and care to the flock of God. We see such an example in the church at Ephesus. Paul called for these elders and instructed them, "Keep watch over yourselves and all the flock of which the Holy Spirit has made you overseers. Be shepherds of the Church of God, which He bought with his own blood" (Acts 20:28). Notice, it was God who made them overseers to watch over the flock.

The churches in the New Testament were led by a plurality of leaders called elders, as it was in Ephesus.[51] Among the team of leaders, there was mutual respect and recognition of each man's authority. Like James in the Jerusalem church, however, there was a lead elder that led the team (Acts 15:13-22). In today's church culture, that person is often called the senior pastor. However, the word "pastor" is only used one time in the Bible as a noun, yet it is used in the present-day church for all the ministry leaders. Other times the word pastor is used in scripture it is a verb. It refers to the job responsibility to feed the flock. Even though the term pastor is used in the modern-day church, those leaders may actually be one of the other five gifts of Ephesians 4:11 such as apostle, prophet, evangelist, teacher.

What Is an Elder?

The elders of the New Testament church were the shepherds, overseers, or leaders who had charge of the flock. They were the regular teachers of the congregation who had the responsibility to equip the people.

The Greek word *presbuteros* denotes stature by comparison of age, maturity, or authority. The term *elder* refers to the person. This term was used regarding the leaders of the synagogue who were more mature. The early church adopted the same term in referring to those who served in giving oversight, care, leadership, and instruction.

---

51 Acts 14:23; 15:2, 4, 6, Philippians 1:1; Acts 13:1

What Does an Elder Do?

The job description of an elder is two-fold, to pastor and bishop. Peter, an apostle who also served as an elder, gives us a summary of these responsibilities.

> *To the elders among you, I appeal as a fellow elder, a witness of Christ's sufferings and one who also will share in the glory to be revealed: Be shepherds of God's flock that is under your care, serving as overseers—not because you must, but because you are willing, as God wants you to be; not greedy for money, but eager to serve; not lording it over those entrusted to you, but being examples to the flock.* (1 Peter 5:1-3)

In this passage, Peter tells the elders to do two things: (1) Pastor or shepherd the flock. The word *shepherd* is translated from the Greek word *poimaino* (poy-mah'-ee-no), which means to feed, rule, or tend the sheep. (2) Bishop or oversee the flock. This means to look diligently over or to take oversight. The job description of an elder is to pastor and bishop. Both of these reflect the ministry of Jesus. Pastoring includes the care and feeding aspect while bishoping involves protecting and warning against sin by giving oversight to people's souls. Elders are to perform these responsibilities willingly with a servant's heart and free from authoritarianism.

Who Can Serve as An Elder?

Church leaders in the New Testament who served in the job description of an elder functioned in one of the five gifts of an apostle, prophet, evangelist, pastor, or teacher. Examples include Peter, an apostle who served as an elder in Jerusalem as well as prophets and teachers in the church at Antioch (1 Peter 5:1; Acts 13:1). These all served in the role of an elder, which included teaching and feeding the flock of God (Acts 11:26).

Therefore, the prerequisite for being an elder is to be called and given to the church as one of the five gifts in Ephesians. In addition to the grace of God, moral and ministry requirements are spelled out in 1 Timothy 3 and Titus 1. There are at least sixteen qualifications listed for elders. These include being above reproach, blameless, the husband of one wife, temperate, self-controlled, prudent, respectable, hospitable, a good teacher, not given to drunkenness, gentle, not quarrelsome, not a lover of money, rules his house well, not a new Christian, and well spoken of outside the church (1 Tim 3:1-7).

Elders are not just selected by other leaders or by a vote of the people. God calls them and they are proven through time and service as qualified to be ordained in that particular local church. The process of selection includes the following essential elements:

1. **A personal response to the call and gift of God.** The individual must know personally that God has called him or her to one of the five gifts of Ephesians 4:11. This a prerequisite for the grace to equip others.

2. **Evidence and fruit of a gift among the congregation.** This gift must be evident among the members of the congregation by the fruit of their labor.

3. **A willingness to work and submit to someone else.** To have authority, one must be under authority. Anyone who is to serve as an elder must be submitted to the vision and not to their own agenda.

4. **A demonstrated willingness to care for people.** Discipleship and care for others is a must for an elder to earn the authority needed to give oversight.

5. **A confirmation of their gift through prophets and apostles.** Elders are not to be selected by the other elders alone, but from the evidence of the congregation and by confirming prophetic words of the presbytery (1 Timothy 4:14).

6. **A level of respect and authority among the people.** An elder must be able to stand before the people with spiritual authority of his own so that when he speaks, he stands as a representative of God. This takes time for this level of respect to be evident. This comes from carrying the load of care and functioning in this capacity.

Deacon, the Second Office in the Church

There are only two offices in the church, the office of the bishop or elder and that of the deacon. The office of the deacon serves the congregation in delegated authority under the elders and has the primary care for the social welfare of the people. They assist the elders in caring for the church. They carry out directives and vision that is set by the elders. Deacons have at least eight qualifications including; worthy of respect, not double-tongued, not addicted to wine, not lovers of money, wholehearted followers of Christ, tested by doing other jobs, husband of one wife, and good managers of their home. Women who serve as deacons or the wives of the deacons must be dignified, not gossipers, temperate, and faithful to what they do (1 Timothy 3:8-12).

Deacons were chosen in Acts 6 to have three primary qualifications, being full of the Holy Spirit, full of wisdom, and faith. These requirements are essential because of the responsibilities given to deacons to lead and superintend the practical needs of the people. These areas of ministry are more than setting up tables for a fellowship dinner. These acts of ministry include visiting the sick, widows and orphans, and taking care of the flock. Many of modern day pastoral duties are in fact deacon ministry. The deacons of the New Testament were powerful spiritual leaders such as Philip, an evangelist who did many miracles and saw the gospel go forth. The first martyr of the early church was the deacon, Stephen.

Application

1. The churches in the New Testament were led by a _____ of leaders, as it was in Ephesus.

2. What is an elder?

   _____

   _____

   _____

3. The responsibilities of an elder are two-fold. Identify each and explain each.

   1) _____

      _____

   2) _____

      _____

4. When we look at the New Testament, we find no church leader who served as an elder who did not function in one of the five gifts of Ephesians 4:11. List here _____, _____, _____, _____, and _____.

5. What are the six essential elements to identifying those who could qualify as elders?

   1) _____

   2) _____

   3) _____

   4) _____

   5) _____

   6) _____

6. What are the two offices in the church?

   1) _____

   2) _____

Every Member Gifted

It is a wonderful revelation to know that each Christian has a unique and authorized place in the Church according to what God has determined. The Bible tells us that each member has been placed in the Body of Christ as it has pleased God (1 Corinthians 12:18). That tells us a couple of things. One, we each have a valuable place of ministry, and two, we can be excited and content about the spiritual gifts given to us since they are from God. Paul writes,

> *We have different gifts, according to the grace given us. If a man's gift is prophesying, let him use it in proportion to his faith. If it is serving, let him serve; if it is teaching, let him teach; if it is encouraging, let him encourage; if it is contributing to the needs of others, let him give generously; if it is leadership, let him govern diligently; if it is showing mercy, let him do it cheerfully.* (Romans 12:6-8)

Here Paul identifies seven gifts, indicating that each member has one or more. These gifts are often called "gifts of function" or "personal ministry gifts," because they reside with the believer and help define each member's function in the church. The nine gifts of the Holy Spirit, called manifestations of the Spirit in 1 Corinthians 12, are different in that they do not reside with the believer, but are given as the Holy Spirit wills (1 Corinthians 12:11). The "functional gifts" are considered different from the five gifts of Christ in Ephesians 4:11. The scripture there is clear, "He gave some to be apostles, and some to be prophets…" Those are individuals given as Christ's gifts themselves for equipping the body of Christ for ministry. In Romans 12, the gifts are given to each member to minister to one another.

Personal Ministry Gifts

Your spiritual gift will be with you for life, for the most part, determining your function as a disciple. Spiritual gifts are not natural talents or acquired skills. Dr. J. Robert Clinton, in his book, *Unlocking Your Giftedness*, identifies a person's "giftedness set as a threefold collection of giftedness elements: natural abilities, acquired skills, and spiritual gifts. Natural abilities refer to those capacities, skills, talents or aptitudes, which are innate in a person and allow him/her to accomplish things."[52] Acquired skills refer to those same capacities. However, these capacities have been learned by a person. A spiritual gift is a God-given unique capacity through which each member ministers. With each member having a gift, God's various graces are manifested through His church when that gift is used to serve others (1

---

52 J. Robert Clinton, Richard W. Clinton, *Unlocking Your Giftedness, What Leaders Need to Know to Develop Themselves and Others* (Altadena, CA: Barnabas Publishers, 1998), 40.

Peter 4:10). As you learn your gift, you will be able to focus more clearly on the purpose of God for your life. It will assist you with priorities and give you a sense of belonging.

Seven Ministry Gifts

These seven gifts serve to identify strengths in each member. All of them are greatly needed and are necessary. Listed below are some benefits and cautions related to each gift.

Prophecy—To bring forth inspired utterances that speak of the will of God or foretells the plans of God. Some associate this gift of prophecy in Romans 12 with prophetic insight apart from a manifestation of the Spirit as in 1 Corinthians 12. That makes sense because these gifts are separate from manifestations of the Spirit. Seen in that light, it gives place for the prophetic ministry in members without one necessarily being a prophet. Sometimes individuals who have this gift will often claim they see things black and white, or right or wrong, with no middle ground. While this trait can be admirable, we must remember these are spiritual gifts and are neither a justification for immaturity in dealing with others nor personality traits. This gift includes prophesying as well as calling for the presence of God to be manifest in the church.

Serving—To minister to the needs and goals of another by using their talents and abilities with joy. A person with this gift can see the needs of others and is willing to undergird his work at his own cost with a sense of joy. A person with this gift must balance their serving and not exclude their own family. They find joy and energy in serving others.

Teaching—The ability to explain truth clearly and succinctly, so others can understand. A person with this gift loves to study and enjoys taking the time to explain truth systematically. A person with this gift may become frustrated with others who can't see the truth, as they see it. This person must also guard against the pride of knowledge.

Exhortation—The ability to come alongside and encourage and comfort others. A person with this gift can discern where people are and have a strong motivation to see others realize their potential. They often focus on making truth practical and inspiring. Someone with this gift may need to guard against having others depend upon them. It is possible for a person with the gift of exhortation to try to lift up those whom they think are discouraged, when in fact, the dealings of God are on them. This gift is very strengthening to others.

Giving—The ability to give resources with great faith and joy. A person with this gift loves to give quality gifts that meet needs as answered prayer. They recognize the prompting of the Spirit to give and can see God at work through their giving. A person with this gift may be tempted to see giving as their primary ministry, and not move into being personally involved with people.

Leading/Administration—The ability to organize and see the steps necessary to accomplish the mission. This gift provides the ability to visualize the task, break it down into smaller tasks, and motivate others. A person with this gift may tend to be more task-oriented than people-oriented.

Showing Mercy—The ability to identify people's spiritual and personal needs with the motivation to extend help. People with this gift are regularly drawn to people who are hurting, and they are moved to take action. Someone with this gift may tend to take on the feelings of others, which may cause the server to pick up an offense. A person with this gift may need to guard against showing pity when tough love is appropriate.

Discover Your Gift

You can discover your spiritual gifts best by being active in a local church and being available to serve people. The first step to discovering your gift is to be familiar with each gift. Second, check your passions. If you could do what you wanted to do in ministering to others, what would that be? Next, become submerged in serving others. It is difficult to determine a particular type of seed, but once it is planted and cultivated, the fruit from that seed will reveal its type. So it is with your gifts. As you serve, others will recognize your gifts by benefiting from them. As you grow in ministry, eventually leaders will help confirm your gift. The best way to discover your gift is by giving your life to others by what comes more naturally to you. There you, and others will find your gift.

You may also find it helpful to take a spiritual gift profile. There are many such profiles that could help you get started in identifying your gifts. Remember, these types of tests are based on ministry experience, so it would be helpful for you to have at least a working knowledge of the gifts if possible. Meet with your mentor and receive input on your gift-mix.[53]

---

53 *Gift-mix*—a label that J. Robert Clinton has given to the set of spiritual gifts being used by a leader at any given time in his/her ministry.

Application

1. We know we have been placed in the Body of Christ as it has pleased God. What two things does this tell us?

   _____

2. What are natural abilities?

   _____

3. What are acquired skills?

   _____

4. What is a spiritual gift?

   _____

5. List each of the seven functional gifts in Romans 12.

   1) _____

   2) _____

   3) _____

   4) _____

   5) _____

   6) _____

   7) _____

6. Which of the seven gifts do you think that you have? Identify the top three that fit you best.

   1) _____

   2) _____

   3) _____

7. Receive a gift profile from your mentor or instructor. Fill it out and see what it says about your spiritual gifts.

Every Member a Minister

There is no greater fulfillment in life than serving in the Master's kingdom. Each person has a part to play. For centuries the church has been divided into two groups, clergy, and layman. Now God has begun to take down that wall of separation. The healthiest churches around the world are those in which all members are encouraged to become active in their gifts.

Who are the Ministers?

In the early church, every member was considered a minister. Peter tells us that the people are a royal priesthood (1 Peter 2:9). In yesterday's lesson, we studied where Paul said that each one has a ministry function. Therefore, every member is a minister.

It is common to refer to members of the church as a layman. This is an Old Testament term used to refer to those who cannot participate in the holy things of God.[54] When members are seen as non-ministers; then only the hired professionals are perceived as capable of doing ministry. Thus, the separation between clergy and layman is established. We must guard against this traditional means of separating leaders and members. In rejecting an artificial division between clergy and laity, we are not saying there should not be great respect given to elders who labor in the Word. The Bible plainly teaches that we are to submit to those who are in authority over us and to esteem them highly in love for the sake of the work (1 Thessalonians 5:12, 13). However, these leaders should be more appropriately seen as coaches and the members as players who have been trained and equipped for participation. Too often the modern church sees their leaders as ministers and leaves everyone else out.

In the Gospels, we read that Jesus chose fishermen and ordinary individuals to be the foundational apostles of His church. In the Book of Acts, we see people like Philip, Barnabas, and Stephen who were regular people equipped in the local church and did mighty works of ministry. Therefore, the local church should be the training center where ordinary people are developed to serve under the elders as ministers of the Gospel.

New Testament ministry includes winning people to Christ, developing them in ministry, and releasing them to responsibilities and oversight for others. That should be our goal in the church today; members are growing in their gifts and fully functioning in the local church as followers of Christ. That is called making disciples of Jesus, to which we are all called.

---

54 Layman—others besides the priest. *New American Standard Translation*, Numbers 1:51; 16:40; Exodus 29:33; Leviticus 22:13

What Is Ministry?

The word ministry is translated from the word serve or servant. The Greek word *diakonia* (dee-ak-on-ee'-ah) means to attend (as a servant) or to aid in Christian service. The Greek word *diakonos* (dee-ak'-on-os) is where we get the word *deacon*. To minister is to serve in and through one's spiritual gift.

As you take on responsibilities, you learn to identify your gift and look for opportunities that fit your area. A willingness to serve regardless of the area, however, is paramount to developing one in ministry. It is in these tasks that one develops. There are many ministry tasks[55] in the church that may or may not be within a person's particular gifting or calling but they are important, nevertheless, to developing faithfulness in the disciple.

Unfortunately, many Christians see ministry as a glamorous and public presentation. They often talk about the future as though one day they will be in ministry. These Christians are looking more for a position than they are a biblical ministry. They fail to discern the body of Christ and the value of every member as a minister. They may see the daily care of young disciples as an interruption to their agenda, thus missing true ministry.

Ministry in the church is primarily winning the lost, assimilating new Christians into the life of the Church, discipling them into maturity, and mobilizing them into service. Unless one is mentoring and discipling others or supporting others who are, then he has not entered New Testament ministry. Ministry is about people. People matter to God, and that is what matters. Christ's church is made up of people, and those who submerge themselves in and among people will be the ministers in the Church.

Developing in Ministry

Ministry comes out of being. You cannot take others where you have not been. You cannot impart to others what you do not have, and you cannot deliver effectively what has not transformed you. There is a difference in giving information and sharing transformation.

Ministry flows out of maturity. Maturity grows out of experiences and accurately relating to God and His Word in life situations. It is during challenging circumstances when one matures the most. A disciple must recognize the learning process and gather wisdom from every setback. Then he will always mature.

---

55 J. Robert Clinton defines as *ministry task* as an assignment from God, which primarily tests a person's faithfulness and obedience but often also allows use of ministry gifts in the context of a task, which has closure, accountability, and evaluation.

There are five practical steps you can take to develop in ministry.

1. **Acknowledge and accept your placement**—Many people are always looking toward the future for ministry while failing to recognize the place in which they reside. Accept where God has placed you in the local church to develop. Also, acknowledge and accept your spiritual gifts as God has given them to you. Bloom where you are planted.

2. **Submit to the vision of where you are planted**—Apply yourself to support the vision of the church where you are planted. Lay down your agenda and become consumed with developing under someone else. Accept ministry tasks when the leaders ask you. Go through the foundation classes and training to become involved in your church. Pray for the leadership and support them with your whole heart.

3. **Commit to the spiritual formations[56] in your life**—Allow adverse situations to develop and grow you. Learn through these times. Apply yourself to character development and your inner-life in Christ. Learn the power of God's presence through prayer and fasting. Learn to hear the voice of the Holy Spirit and establish a regular time in the Word of God.

4. **Ask for help with ministry skills**—Be willing to be mentored. Don't expect anyone to give you all his time, but determine what you can receive from those around you. Write out where you see they can help you and ask for that help. Seek input from others on how you can develop and improve your people skills, communication skills, and leadership skills. Apply yourself to reading and studying in the areas in which you need development the most. Develop further in your gifts.

5. **Seek fruit that will remain**—At the end of your life, what will matter the most are the people in whom you have invested your life. Determine now that you will disciple others into what you are learning. Your ministry development is in direct proportion to the people whom you have helped in their ministry. When you help enough people reach their potential, your leadership influence will have grown exponentially. The test of a mature disciple is when those he has discipled are making disciples. That is fruit that will remain.

---

56 J. Robert Clinton's book *Leadership Perspectives* defines *spiritual formation* as the development of the inner-life of a person of God so that the person experiences more of the life of Christ, reflects more Christi-like characteristics in personality and in everyday relationships, and increasingly knows the power and presence of Christ in ministry.

Application

1. What does the word layman mean?

_____

_____

2. Why should we guard against separating the church into two groups of people, clergy and layman?

_____

_____

3. Who should be seen as the ministers in the church?

_____

_____

4. Define the word ministry.

_____

_____

5. What is a ministry task?

_____

_____

6. Ministry in the church is primarily _____ the lost, _____ new Christians into the life of the church, _____ them into maturity, and _____ them into service.

7. List the five steps to developing into ministry.

   1) _____

   2) _____

   3) _____

   4) _____

   5) _____

Overcoming Conflict

Most people know of someone who at one time attended church; however, they say they no longer attend church because they got hurt. Whether that is the full story or not we will never know, but one thing is likely: most of these conflicts will never be resolved, and the real problem never discovered. This points to the need for a church to have intentional conflict resolution. Intentional conflict resolution is one of the keys to a healthy church. That is why this week's lessons will attempt to bring light as to how conflict arises and how to resolve it.

Peace is not the absence of conflict, but a byproduct of a willingness to resolve disputes. The church is called to demonstrate a redemptive community where individuals can learn to grow in spite of differences. Harmony does not come from conformity, but rather from an appreciation of unique distinctions. Therefore, the aim for peace is not to avoid conflict, but rather to work through conflict.

An unhealthy view of conflict can result in seeds of division. A weak concept of mercy and love that shuns confrontation, often bears worse fruit. In the name of tolerance or maturity, some people attempt to evade necessary resolutions, thus producing the very trauma they sought to avoid. Only by a healthy view of conflict will a church grow into maturity.

Preserving unity is a goal, but the process is vital. When someone responds out of their weakness and fear rather than healthy love, then peace is eventually lost. While instructing the church in Rome to live in harmony, Paul says, "If it is possible, as far as it depends on you, live at peace with everyone" (Romans 12:18). From this admonition we discover that it may not be possible to have peace; however, as far as you are concerned, you must take the proper steps and do your part.

The Holy Spirit produces unity, and that unity is kept through humility, gentleness, and longsuffering of the saints. So, while it becomes imperative that Christ's disciples learn how to resolve conflict, it must be done through the aspects of the fruit of the Spirit.

Reconciling an Offended Brother

Let's address one of the first concepts of conflict resolution: owning your sin. Of course, it goes without saying that your first response is to God; however, the Scripture says that when one goes to worship and then remembers that a brother has a case against him, he must address it immediately before further worship. Jesus put reconciliation above our worship when he said,

Therefore, if you are offering your gift at the altar and there remember that your brother has something against you, leave your gift there in front of the altar. First, go and be reconciled to your brother; then come and offer your gift. (Matthew 5:23, 24)

God sees the need for reconciliation as such a priority that even worship does not take precedent. In the holy presence of God, in humble worship, the Holy Spirit can remind us of any offenses that have not been resolved. This requires immediate action. Go and reconcile or make the situation different between you and the offended brother.

This principle works when a brother is offended at you for no apparent reason. However, the context of this instruction does not refer to unknown or hidden offenses but rather a known case. Notice, Jesus said, "If you are offering your gift at the altar and there remember." This refers to a known offense that has been overlooked or forgotten by the offending brother, but in the presence of God, the offender remembers that he has a case against him. Now that he remembers, God, Himself holds him accountable. He must act obediently. This concept works for all Christians and should be used by couples in marriage as well. For those who are married, they are first Christians before they are married partners.

How to Ask Forgiveness

One of the greatest characteristics of a disciple is the willingness to own transgressions. To humble oneself and accept wrong words or actions is a great virtue. Much damage has occurred because the offending brother has not understood the process of seeking forgiveness from someone else. How one approaches another seeking forgiveness sets the tone and maybe the outcome of reconciliation.

First, the one seeking forgiveness should have a clear understanding of his sin. If it is a situation where that has not been clarified, then an open heart is necessary to identify with the offended brother. If in fact, it is a "remembered" sin, then the offender will know. To have a clear understanding of the sin is to know how God sees it and how it has offended the other brother. Identify with the pain that the sin has caused. See it from the other person's perspective.

Second, go to the brother prepared to repent regardless of his response. Remember, you are only responsible for your actions. If the offended brother fails to offer forgiveness, then God will work on your behalf nevertheless.

Third, do not use the words, "I am sorry." In our English language, those words are used too lightly. Some have used those words with such frivolousness that it has offended even more. For example, the repenting person's tone and attitude with the words, "I am sorry that you were offended," may sound like, "I am sorry that you were so weak and unhealthy that you got offended over something that a normal person would not get offended over." The best approach is to say, "I was wrong!" An example of someone properly repenting would sound like this:

I just want you to know how bad I feel about my actions. I see how wrong I was, and I have been so convicted of it. It grieves me to see how I have hurt you. It was not right. I was wrong. Would you please forgive me?

Wow! Can you imagine the different response that kind of repentance would bring over someone simply saying, "I am sorry if I offended you"?

The desire to justify and preserve ourselves is so strong that it is tempting to put words in the repentance sentence that lessen the feelings of wrong that we are experiencing while repenting. For example, one might say, "I probably should not have done that" or "if I offended you." Leave out words like "if," "maybe," or "probably." Simply own your transgression without justification.

If the offended brother responds inappropriately, it is still imperative that you humble yourself for true reconciliation. God will vindicate you in time. The offended brother may say, "Why have you waited so long to ask forgiveness?" Or he might strike back with, "You just don't know how much that hurt me!" In each situation, we must respond in a Christ-like manner. Simply say, "I can see how this has hurt you; it just shows how deep my sin has been. I was so wrong." By humbling yourself and not becoming defensive, you are allowing the Holy Spirit to work on your behalf. Remember, God sees this attempt on your part as being equal to worship and honoring of Him. Treat it in the same manner.

Application

1. Peace is not the absence of _____ but a byproduct of willingness to _____ disputes.

2. What can come from an unhealthy view of conflict?

   _____

3. God sees the need for _____ to be such a priority that even worship does not take precedent.

4. What is one of the greatest characteristics of a disciple?

   _____

5. When going to another to ask forgiveness, what is the first thing the offender should have clear?

   _____

6. What words should you guard against using when seeking forgiveness from someone?

   _____

7. Write out in your own words an example of what should be said when seeking forgiveness from someone.

   _____

   _____

8. In a desire to justify yourself, it is often tempting to insert certain words while asking forgiveness. Give an example of some of these words.

   _____

   _____

9. What should be your response if the offended brother reacts inappropriately when approached? Write out an example of what you can use if this ever happens to you.

   _____

   _____

Confronting A Brother

Very few people like confrontation. In fact, it is so few that I have never met anyone who admitted to liking it, but mature disciples know the valuable fruit it brings. Healthy dialogue is necessary for peace to flourish. A failure to interact with another out of weakness or fear can only produce conflict later.

What is Confrontation?

Defining confrontation may help in embracing its value. One meaning of the word confrontation is, "a face to face meeting." A common definition is the "clashing of two forces." Both could be accurate, but let's address it from a biblical view, that is, "admonishing, warning, or instructing one another." Paul wrote to the Romans expressing his confidence in their knowledge and love for one to instruct each other. He wrote, "I myself am convinced, my brothers, that you yourselves are full of goodness, complete in knowledge and competent to instruct one another" (Romans 15:14). The word translated "instruct" is also translated as "admonish" and "warn." Instructing the church how to deal with an unruly member, Paul commands them to "warn him as a brother." This was to be done with love and tenderness, yet firmly. Paul knew the result would end in peace.

> *If anyone does not obey our instruction in this letter, take special note of him. Do not associate with him, in order that he may feel ashamed. Yet do not regard him as an enemy, but warn him as a brother. Now may the Lord of peace Himself give you peace at all times and in every way. The Lord be with all of you.* (2 Thessalonians 3:14-16)

This form of confrontation is not an assault or judgment on another's character, but rather a gentle warning by the authority of the Scriptures. The Word of God is the authority that one believer has with another. Confronting someone with your own opinion or judgment will produce death and not life. Paul spoke of producing a pleasant, peaceful end.

How Do You Confront?

What did Paul know about the need to admonish a wayward brother that would bring peace? And why did Jesus instruct us to go to a brother who has sinned against you? What is the wisdom and benefit of obeying the Lord's instruction to us in this matter? Answers to these questions must but be sought. Jesus taught us how to deal with sin in the Church. He taught,

If your brother sins against you, go and show him his fault, just between the two of you. If he listens to you, you have won your brother over. But if he will not listen, take one or two others along, so that "every matter may be established by the testimony of two or three witnesses." If he refuses to listen to them, tell it to the church; and if he refuses to listen even to the church, treat him as you would a pagan or a tax collector. (Matthew 18:15-17)

Jesus gives us detailed instruction on what to do when a brother sins against another.

1. For biblical confrontation to work, the person being approached must be a brother in the Lord. We as believers are not called to address those who are outside of the church (1 Corinthians 5:9, 10).

2. The one who has been sinned against must take the initiative to approach the other. Don't wait for them to see their sin, lest it becomes a stumbling block of bitterness for you.

3. You must go alone. At this point, it is a must that you have not talked to anyone else at all. If you do, you will corrupt the process.

4. You must show him his fault. It is important that you not judge his actions or his character; only address the action. For example, "I want to talk about what you said earlier today. I heard you say . . ." Don't pile on guilt by stating how much it hurt you or how others are talking about what he said. Simply tell him his sin. Don't say, "You were mean to me." Speak about the actual action. Have Scripture available to show it is a sin, such as "false testimony," etc. The reason this is important is that many times our feelings are hurt because someone does not do what we wanted them to do. They may not have sinned against us, but rather they failed to meet our expectations. That is different and should not be addressed.

5. Make sure it is a sin that was committed against you. If it was against another, God must give you entrance by authority or relationship.

6. If your brother hears you, then you have won or gained a brother. At this point, it is over and should not be shared with any others. Love covers a multitude of sin.

7. If he does not hear you, then take one or two others. It is at this point where most people defile this process of confrontation. It is critical that the one or two people you take with you have NOT HEARD anything about this situation. If you tell them what it is about, you are guilty of gossip and tampering with the jury. Simply ask them if they would go with you to hear a matter in which you desire to have reconciliation. They should hear it for the first time in front of the offending brother.

8. The matter is told again in the same way to the offending brother, but this time it is in front of one or two witnesses. Explain to the offending brother that the witnesses have no idea of the matter that you are about to discuss. If the witnesses determine that a sin has not been committed, then your response is to graciously receive that judgment and be reconciled based on the decision. If they

agree with your assessment and the offending brother hears and repents, then be reconciled and the matter is dropped with no further discussion.

9. If he does not hear you, then you should go to the leadership of the church, stating succinctly the situation and outcome. Then allow the leadership to question both you and the witnesses separately. If you and the witness confirm the transgression and response, then it will be taken to the church body.

10. Before it is taken to the church body, the offending member must know each step that is being taken and be invited to be present in order that repentance takes place. The process and situation should be written down and given by the leadership of the church with nothing added or discussed further.

11. The unrepentant brother is to be treated as an unbeliever, which is with compassion that eventually he would repent. Members should remain kind and civil but realize this brother has removed himself by his refusal to repent.

It is within this context that Jesus says, "Whatever you bind on earth is bound in heaven, and whatever you loose on earth is loosed in heaven." (Matthew 18:18-20). He is speaking of the governmental authority of the church. He promises to be in the midst of two or three when they are involved in such matters.

If done appropriately, repentance will probably come early in the exchange of these steps. Remember, confrontation is for redemption and not punishment. All the above encounters must be done in gentleness and with consideration, manifesting the love of Christ (Galatians 6:1).

Application

1. In your own words, give a biblical definition to confrontation.

    _____

    _____

2. The Word of God is the _____ that one believer has with another. Confronting someone with your own _____ or judgment will produce death and not life.

3. In your own words, give the eleven steps to carrying out the instructions that Jesus gives to go to a brother who has sinned against you.

    1) _____

    2) _____

    3) _____

    4) _____

    5) _____

    6) _____

    7) _____

    8) _____

    9) _____

    10) _____

    11) _____

Wisdom in Relationships

One of the greatest values we have in life is our relationship with other believers. Unfortunately, many Christians may not see the true worth of these relationships. That is why Paul wrote the Ephesians and instructed them to make every effort to keep the unity of the Spirit through the bond of peace (Ephesians 4:3). He talks about giving intensive effort to preserve what the Holy Spirit brings forth. The words "bond of peace" refers to a "peaceful union, where the interests of all parties are concentrated, cemented, and sealed; the Spirit of God being the seal upon this knot."[57]

There are a few common sense and wisdom-based concepts that we should discuss that will help you with relationships and keep the bond of peace.

Sins vs. Hurts

The Bible says, "If your brother sins against you, go and show him his fault" (Matt 8:15). There are times when a person may be offended or hurt, but in reality, no sin has occurred. This requires a different approach to a resolution. It is important to note that many hurts come out of unmet expectations. When expectations are placed upon another beyond what the other person has committed, then an offense will no doubt arise. The hurt person may expect certain actions or behaviors because he considers it normal, or because the other person has responded a certain way in times past. In this situation, the injured individual does not have a biblical right to be offended. It reveals a need or lack in his life that must be healed and turned over to God. This is not a legitimate sin and should not be addressed in the same manner. Even though the wounded individual's perception is true to him, and his hurt is a reality, this situation must be approached differently.

A good question to ask is, "Was the law of God broken by the offending brother?" Since sin is the transgression of the law, a biblical offense may not have occurred. If the hurt has come because the injured person has formed a wrong judgment, unfair expectation, or is overly sensitive, the offended individual can find help without confrontation. The wounded individual should take it to God in prayer, releasing it in an exchange with Christ. Jesus suffered in every manner so, He can identify with the hurting. That person must give it to Jesus and receive His love and healing. During the exchange, the individual may discover from which past experiences these expectations and hurts have risen. This is an opportunity to receive a deeper work in his life. Later, when the wounded individual is healed from the situation, then a healthy conversation can develop and suggestions made to the offending brother on how to

---

57 Adam Clarke Commentary

better show appreciation or care. This will enhance the relationship and not damage it. Since a different approach is being used, it is important not to point out the past hurt at this time.

Many offenses have increased through lack of wisdom. When an individual is hurting, he may feel justified in saying whatever he pleases. I have seen individuals go to another who has no idea of any past hurts. They were told, "Brother, I have hated you for years," or "I was so offended at you for such a long time, and I just wanted to come and tell you that I forgive you." The hurt individual may think he is doing the right thing because of his past wound, but in reality, he may be causing hurt or distrust. It does not benefit either party to express past anger, hatred, or dislike when there is no particular sin matter to discuss. A non-sinful offense is best addressed in the offended brother's heart. He should take it to God and God alone.

On the other hand, if actions are ongoing or the hurt from a true sinful offense, then a proper approach should be taken to address the actual behavior. For example, it should be said, "I would like to talk to you about several events that have taken place in which I was directly involved. Here is what I observed . . . were you aware of it? This caused me pain, as it was a judgment against my character, etc., . . ." By stating what you observed or citing an incident, it allows for proper confrontation without judgment.

Your Liberty vs. Your Brother

Another responsibility of Christians is to walk in love to not cause a brother to stumble. Paul, the apostle, gives a very good example of our liberty verses our brother in 1 Corinthians 8 and Romans 14. Here he addresses the issue of meat that has been offered to idols. In the Corinthian culture, idols, and temples to idols, were as common as restaurants are in our day. Quality meat could be obtained free or at a great discount since it had already been used in the pagan temple. Part of the social aspect of the community was to go and eat at the temples. This was a place for those who normally could not afford meat. Some Christians did not consider it a sin to take advantage of the available meat since they themselves did not practice idolatry and false gods were not gods at all. They figured their freedom in Christ was sufficient, and the meat was acceptable. Other Christians contended that to even be associated with the meat connected with idolatry was showing support for, and participating in, the worship of false gods. Paul's advice was to agree with the Corinthians in that the false gods were not gods at all and to speak of his liberty to be able to eat such foods if it was offered. However, he takes a strong stand against using his liberty in front of another Christian if it would cause them to question their faith, or go back into idolatry. He wrote, "Therefore, if what I eat causes my brother to fall into sin, I will never eat meat again, so that I will not cause him to fall" (1 Corinthians 8:13).

He tells us in Romans to pursue the things that make for peace and the building up of one another. Do not tear down the work of God for the sake of food (Romans 14:19, 20).

There are many modern-day examples that fit this situation. Once such example is the drinking of wine or beer. In some countries, it is quite acceptable among the Christians in the society to drink wine at meals and to have a cold beer while in some other situations it is considered compromising with the world. While the Bible speaks out against being drunk and turning to strong drink for consolation, it is a matter of conscience and liberty if one does not get drunk.[58] This is where Paul's warning is appropriate. If a Christian's liberty to drink influenced a new convert to go back into a sinful lifestyle, then it would not only be sinning against that brother but against Christ Himself (1 Corinthians 8:12).

Though one may have a clear conscience, that in and of itself does not make it an acceptable practice at all times. Some may reject Paul's warning with this judgment, "Those Christians are just too narrow-minded and legalistic! I am going to do what I like; I have liberty in Christ." Such an attitude reveals a lack of love for the body of Christ, and self-centeredness. This attitude will not preserve the unity of the Spirit. Let us walk in our liberty, but not use it to bring an offense to another.

---

58 Ephesians 5:18; 1 Peter 4:3; Galatians. 5:21; Romans 13:13; Proverbs 23:31-32

Application

1. Name three ways in which a brother in the Lord may be hurt and it not be a true sinful offense.

   1) _____

   2) _____

   3) _____

2. If there is not a true sinful act against you, yet you are hurt by unfair expectations, wrong judgments, or an oversensitivity, how should you handle this situation?

   _____

   _____

   _____

   _____

3. In your own words, explain why it is important to have a specific event or sinful act to address when going to another brother who has offended you?

   _____

   _____

   _____

4. Give an example, other than what is in the lesson, of being careful not to take personal Christian liberties to cause another brother to stumble.

   _____

   _____

   _____

   _____

5. Meditate on this week's memory verses. (See appendix.)

Words of Conflict

King Solomon wrote, "Reckless words pierce like a sword, but the tongue of the wise brings healing" (Proverbs 12:18). Conflict or comfort may come from your words. Changing your words may transform your life as well as the lives of others. What you say, and how you say it, can have a powerful influence on your relationships and your leadership with others.

Studies have shown that body language and tone of voice have a greater influence upon our communication than what we say, yet words have the power of life and death. Proverbs tells us, "The tongue has the power of life and death, and those who love it will eat its fruit" (Proverbs 18:21).

Words are powerful. Nathaniel Hawthorne once said, "Words—so innocent and powerless as they are, as standing in a dictionary, how potent for good and evil they become in the hands of one who knows how to combine them."[59]

Loose Words

A loose word that gives momentary laughter to others at the expense of another, can create a conflict that lasts for years. King David said, "Your tongue is like a sharpened razor" (Psalms 52:2), and before you know it, you can cause great damage. A wisecrack or "friendly" ridicule may appear to be good camaraderie, but in the end, it brings friction and conflict. Trust builds a bond of peace, and it is difficult to establish trust when one is fearful of being slapped with words.

The Scriptures declare, "Whoever would love life and see good days must keep his tongue from evil and his lips from deceitful speech" (1 Peter 3:10). It is a benefit to all parties when one keeps his tongue from evil. If you love life and enjoy peace, then it pays to guard your words.

People often feel freer to speak cruel words to family members or those who are closest to them. Though it may appear to be overlooked by their family, it costs them more regarding closeness and real trust in their relationships. It can be years before the full evidence of family wounds from words be revealed.

Evidence of the fruit of the Spirit working in us or the lack thereof is how we guard our tongue. James wrote, "If anyone considers himself religious and yet does not keep a tight rein on his tongue, he deceives himself and his religion is worthless" (James 1:26).

---

59 Hilary Rich, Irwin Katsof, Chain Feld, *The Words Can Heal Handbook* (Baltimore, MD: Leviathan Press, 2002), 7.

Gossiping Words

A report of a personal nature is defined as gossip. If the report does not edify or compliment the person, then it certainly should be considered gossip. It matters not if the report is true, it still constitutes gossip. Gossip injures the victim, the hearer, and the one who is the gossiper.

The reason that gossip has such lure is that it satisfies the soul of man. Solomon wrote, "The words of a gossip are like choice morsels; they go down to a man's inmost parts" (Proverbs 18:8). It makes the listener and the gossiper feel better about their stature. It gives them a sense of being on the inside of information. It gives a sense of control and being ahead of others. It often comes out of vented anger, and revenge, or jealousy, thus it feels satisfying to the gossiper.

There are many things people tell themselves to make an excuse for their gossip. They may say, "Well, it is true," or "I would say this if they were right here," or maybe, "I wouldn't mind if someone said that about me" and "We are friends; I can say this." No excuse makes gossip right or non-damaging. The Bible tells us, "Whoever repeats a matter separates friends" (Proverbs 17:9).

For gossip to continue, there must be someone who will listen to gossip. Gossipers can be identified first as gossip listeners. These people will ask certain questions in the hope of gathering information about others; before long a morsel of gossip is shared between the two parties. The best way to stop gossip is to not participate with the gossiper. Silence only condones the sin of gossip. Being a willing listener is another way to spread gossip. Proverbs declares, "Without wood, a fire goes out; without gossip, a quarrel dies down" (Proverbs 26:20).

Gossip can also be slander. To slander means to speak evil of someone or to say something that puts him or her in a bad light. Paul the Apostle tells Titus to teach the Christians, "to slander no one, to be peaceable and considerate, and to show true humility toward all men" (Titus 3:2).

Judging Words

When you speak badly about people, you will soon not like them. Feelings follow thoughts and words. Conflicts arise because opinions are formed and turned into judgments. James warned us, "Brothers, do not slander one another. Anyone who speaks against his brother or judges him speaks against the law and judges it . . ." (James 4:11).

When a judgment is added to a fact, then it becomes an accusation. For example, if someone fails to speak to you, that would be a fact. To add a judgment would be to say, "They are mad at me; therefore, they did not speak." This immediately causes a conflict and division in your heart toward them.

If a disagreement arises and one person expresses what he understands to be the truth, and the other disagrees, you have a normal disagreement. Such a disagreement is easier to resolve than an accusation.

For instance, if one of the parties in the argument judges the other to be a liar, you now have more than a disagreement; you have judgment.

Calling someone rude, dumb, irresponsible, untrustworthy, or stuck-up will cause feelings for that person to change and expectations from them to follow. We are not allowed to judge motives or read between the lines. We can only address actions or situations that arise.

Judgments are often formed before hearing the entire story. Proverbs tell us a story may seem right until you hear both sides (Proverbs 18:17). Once a judgment is made and repeated to someone else, it causes great harm and destruction.

When Jesus said to not judge in Matthew 7, He speaks of not judging motives and people's hearts. Though the facts may be correct, we are not given the right to judge the motives or intentions. This remains for God to judge. That is true with your own heart. People often say, "You know my heart" or "I did not intend to do that." Paul said that even if his conscience is clear that does not mean he was innocent, but only the Lord can judge our heart (1 Corinthians 4:4).

We are allowed to judge actions as being right or wrong, for the spiritual man judges all things (1 Corinthians 2:15). However, if we enter into judging other's motives and their heart we will experience the judgment of others. Whenever you hear someone regularly speaking of others judging them they might be guilty of that same offense. Jesus said,

> *Do not judge, and you will not be judged. Do not condemn, and you will not be condemned. Forgive, and you will be forgiven. Give, and it will be given to you. A good measure, pressed down, shaken together and running over, will be poured into your lap. For with the measure you use, it will be measured to you.* (Luke 6:37, 38)

When we judge, condemn, or refuse to forgive, we will receive the same in return from others, but it will be pressed down, shaken together, and running over. We reap judgment from our judgments.

Application

1. Reckless words _____ like a sword, but the tongue of the wise brings _____ .

2. Why do you think that Proverbs says that keeping your tongue will help you to have good days and a better life?

   _____

   _____

   _____

3. Define gossip.

   _____

   _____

   _____

4. There cannot be gossipers without those who _____ .

5. When a judgment is added to a fact, then it becomes an _____ .

6. Explain why it is much better to address incidents and actions rather than motives.

   _____

   _____

   _____

7. Meditate on this week's memory verses, and be prepared to recite them in class. (See appendix.)

Words of Healing

It seems everyone can tell you about an event in his life when ugly words were spoken that brought about a deep wound. These hurts often last a lifetime. While words have the power to destroy they also have the power to heal and to edify. These healing words are sweet to the soul and come from a wise heart (Proverbs 16:23, 24).

The Scriptures instruct us to encourage one another. The right words spoken at the right time can bring healing and life. Proverbs tell us, "The tongue that brings healing is a tree of life, but a deceitful tongue crushes the spirit" (Proverbs 15:4). Knowing the power of words will motivate a person to speak healing rather than destructive words. Practice speaking words of healing. Let your words be filled with grace.

The Bible instructs us to be slow to speak and to hold our tongue. Proverbs says, "When words are many, sin is not absent" (Proverbs 10:19). When we talk too much and listen too little, we can fall into the trap of not bringing forth healing words. It is possible to unintentionally wound a friend by sharing what others have said. In an attempt to protect or show support, many have unwisely carried slander. Mark Twain once said, "It takes your enemy and your friend, working together to hurt you to the heart; the one to slander you and the other to get the news to you."[60] To speak healing words, we must weigh our speech very carefully.

Halting Gossip and Slander

One of the best ways to stop gossip is to cancel listeners. If someone says, "Did you hear? And they proceed to tell you gossip, change the subject. Before they have a chance to say anything further, simply change the subject with a question, "How are you doing?"

You can probably tell when someone is about to dump gossip or slander on you. They may use words like, "Don't tell anyone I told you this!" or "Can you keep a secret?" or maybe "You won't believe what I heard today!" Be prepared to deflect these introductions to gossip. You can deflect some gossip simply by changing the subject. For example: "Did you see the dress she wore to church the other day?" You say, "Speaking of clothes, did I ever show you that new outfit that I got?"

Christians often come up with some introductions to gossip that sound benign, such as, "I've just got to talk to someone." Or "We need to be praying for . . ." If they bring up someone in gossip, you can say, "I

---

60 Hilary Rich, Irwin Katsof, Chain Feld, *The Words Can Heal Handbook* (Baltimore, MD: Leviathan Press, 2002) p. 24

would be happy to go with you to talk with them. I can see that this is bothering you, and I know that if you could talk it out, it would help. Why don't we get with them?"

Since gossip is a sin is often important to encourage people to go back to their source and put a stop to the gossip. For example: "Did you hear that so-and-so was seen drunk the other night?" You say, "How do you know that to be true?" The gossiper says, "I heard it from so-and-so." You say, "Even if it is true, it does not benefit us to know. Could we go to that person and ask them not to repeat this to others?"

Speaking Positively

A great way to turn the course of judgmental words is to speak positively about the person who is being criticized. For example, a slandering person might say, "Man, so-and-so seems so odd." You can say, "You know, one of the things that I like about him is how faithful he is to his family." By countering the negative, you will soon establish a clear message that you are not available for slander.

Think about ways in which you can become a world-class encourager. Ask God to show you how to encourage people around you. The best way to have peaceful relationships is to create a healthy environment through encouraging words. By speaking pleasant words, you promote an atmosphere of learning.

People need to hear words that bring healing to their souls. This is not flattery, but true words of life. Flattery is when you say something favorable to another person to get something from them. When you minister with positive words, you are touching a person's soul from the heart of God.

Make an effort to say things like: "I like this about you . . ." or "I admire that about you." Acknowledge areas in which you have seen growth. Let others know when you see how they have been faithful. Complimenting character qualities is a good way to thank people for doing the right thing. This will help break down feelings of jealously or envy in your own life. Seeds of encouragement will eventually come back to you in the same measure you give out. Words written in a note or letter are just as powerful as words spoken. Often, a written note will have a greater impact because of the effort put forth to write the note.

As a disciple, you desire the very presence of God in your life. Healthy relationships come from genuine people of God who love and honor others as themselves. The only time we are instructed to outdo one another is in honoring each other. Paul wrote instructing us to love one another with brotherly affection and outdo one another in showing honor (Romans 12:10).

When Do You Tell?

There may be times when one believer observes another Christian involved in obvious sinful behavior. The first step is to go to that person and ask them if what you saw was correct. It may not be as it seems.

If, in fact, it is a true transgression give them a chance to repent. If they repent, then the matter is covered with love (Proverbs 17:9). It is not to be shared with others.

If the sin is of a nature that endangers a spouse or family member, then with loving firmness and respect, inform them that you will give them the opportunity to tell their spouse within a short period. After that time, you will be obligated to inform the spouse yourself if they do not. That is as far as it can go. This is not slander; rather it is a biblical confrontation with truth. If there still is no repentance the offended spouse may go to the elders of the church. The offended person is free to do so.

Another occasion in which telling something is not gossip, is when someone is speaking confidentially to a counselor or pastor about relationships that directly involve themselves. Even then, a wise counselor will address the one present and not deal with the party who is not in the counseling session.

There are times when leaders who are responsible for an organization or business, have subordinates or employees who bring an offense to others. This can happen in a church. If the offense is in the operation of the ministry or business then someone can bring a complaint against the offender by going to the authority over that individual.

Note: Serious crimes are a different matter. If an individual confesses a serious crime to you, they have burdened you with information that must be addressed. You can give that person the opportunity to confess to authorities, but tell them you will have to inform civil authorities yourself.

Learning to guard your words and speak life to others is key to spiritual influence. Being a safe person so others can trust you, will go a long way in bringing health to relationships. The local church must be a safe place to grow. People need to know they are loved, forgiven, and accepted. This is demonstrated through our words and actions.

Application

1. Write out Proverbs 15:4.

_____

_____

2. Explain Mark Twain's quote on slander.

_____

_____

3. Write out your own deflections to the following gossip starters.

   "Can I tell you something just between you and me?"

   _____

   _____

   "Can you keep a secret?"

   _____

   _____

4. Give an example of a time in your own life where positive words brought great encouragement.

_____

_____

_____

5. Write out several ways that you can encourage others with your words.

_____

_____

_____

_____

Weekly Scripture Memory Verses

Week One - Verse One **Matthew 16:24, 25** Then Jesus said to his disciples, "If anyone would come after me, he must deny himself and take up his cross and follow me. For whoever wants to save his life will lose it, but whoever loses his life for me will find it.	**Week One - Verse Two** **I Job 2:15, 16** Do not love the world or anything in the world. If anyone loves the world, the love of the Father is not in him. For everything in the world—the cravings of sinful man, the lust of his eyes and the boasting of what he has and does—comes not from the Father but from the world.
Week Two - Verse One **1 Corinthians 10:13** No temptation has seized you except what is common to man. And God is faithful; he will not let you be tempted beyond what you can bear. But when you are tempted, he will also provide a way out so that you can stand up under it.	**Week Two - Verse Two** **James 1:14-15** but each one is tempted when, by his own evil desire, he is dragged away and enticed. Then, after desire has conceived, it gives birth to sin; and sin, when it is full-grown, gives birth to death.
Week Three - Verse One **Ephesians 6:12** For our struggle is not against flesh and blood, but against the rulers, against the authorities, against the powers of this dark world and against the spiritual forces of evil in the heavenly realms.	**Week Three - Verse Two** **Colossians 2:15** And having disarmed the powers and authorities, he made a public spectacle of them, triumphing over them by the cross.

Week Four - Verse One **Romans 8:28** And we know that in all things God works for the good of those who love him, who have been called according to his purpose.	**Week Four - Verse Two** **Hebrews 12:1** Therefore, since we are surrounded by such a great cloud of witnesses, let us throw off everything that hinders and the sin that so easily entangles, and let us run with perseverance the race marked out for us.
Week Five - Verse One **Luke 4:18** The Spirit of the Lord is on me because he has anointed me to preach good news to the poor. He has sent me to proclaim freedom for the prisoners and recovery of sight for the blind, to release the oppressed.	**Week Five - Verse Two** **Ephesians 1:7, 8** In him we have redemption through his blood, the forgiveness of sins, in accordance with the riches of God's grace that he lavished on us with all wisdom and understanding.
Week Six - Verse One **James 1:21** Therefore, get rid of all moral filth and the evil that is so prevalent and humbly accept the word planted in you, which can save you.	**Week Six - Verse Two** **Hebrews 4:12** For the Word of God is living and active. Sharper than any double-edged sword, it penetrates even to dividing soul and spirit, joints and marrow; it judges the thoughts and attitudes of the heart.
Week Seven - Verse One **2 Timothy 2:15** Do your best to present yourself to God as one approved, a workman who does not need to be ashamed and who correctly handles the word of truth.	**Week Seven - Verse Two** **James 1:6-8** But when he asks, he must believe and not doubt because he who doubts is like a wave of the sea, blown and tossed by the wind. That man should not think he will receive anything from the Lord; he is a double-minded man, unstable in all he does.

Week Eight - Verse One **Ephesians 3:20** Now to him who is able to do immeasurably more than all we ask or imagine, according to his power that is at work within us,	**Week Eight - Verse Two** **Acts 2:1-4** When the day of Pentecost came, they were all together in one place. Suddenly a sound like the blowing of a violent wind came from heaven and filled the whole house where they were sitting. They saw what seemed to be tongues of fire that separated and came to rest on each of them. All of them were filled with the Holy Spirit and began to speak in other tongues as the Spirit enabled them.
Week Nine - Verse One **Romans 13:1** Everyone must submit himself to the governing authorities, for there is no authority except that which God has established. The authorities that exist have been established by God. Consequently, he who rebels against the authority is rebelling against what God has instituted, and those who do so will bring judgment on themselves.	**Week Nine - Verse Two** **Romans 12:3** For by the grace given me I say to every one of you: Do not think of yourself more highly than you ought, but rather think of yourself with sober judgment, in accordance with the measure of faith God has given you.
Week Ten - Verse One **Matt 5:23, 24** Therefore, if you are offering your gift at the altar and there remember that your brother has something against you, leave your gift there in front of the altar. First go and be reconciled to your brother; then come and offer your gift.	**Week Ten - Verse Two** **Ephesians 4:3** Make every effort to keep the unity of the Spirit through the bond of peace.